ASSERTIVE
COMMUNICATION

THE SECRET TO SPEAKING WITHOUT TALKING
NONSENSE, SAYING NO WITH STYLE AND
MAKING YOUR WORD COUNT GOLD. BECOME A
PERSUASIVE TALKER WITHOUT SHYNESS AND
RAISE YOUR SELF-ESTEEM!

OLLIE SNIDER

THANK YOU FOR READING MY BOOK

This has been my big project for several months (almost a year) and to be honest, it wasn't easy.

It was the closest thing to a roller coaster ride. I have been through the lowest and darkest moments, immersed in fear of not knowing if I was doing it right, but I have also had the privilege of seeing everything from the top and seeing how many people I will probably never have the privilege of meeting can benefit from my small but humble contribution to their lives.

It literally took me months and many sleepless nights to express my knowledge here. I am a person who naturally finds it difficult to express his feelings, but this book allowed me to open my mind and get out of my comfort zone, which is why I thank you for getting to this point in reading.

I would like to take this opportunity to thank my family for the constant support they gave me during this long journey of writing, designing and hours in front of the computer. I couldn't have done it without them. I love them with all my heart.

And before I say goodbye, I'd like to ask you a small favor.

Please enjoy this work. I say goodbye with great gratitude.

Ollie Snider

TABLE OF CONTENTS

INTRODUCTION

"To be passive is to let others decide for you. To be aggressive is to decide for others. To be assertive is to decide for yourself." -Edith Eva Eger-

Assertive communication is so powerful that it is used by FBI detectives, politicians, teachers, salespeople and publicists, among others. It's no exaggeration to say that, if you develop it, you can empower yourself in practically any type of circumstance. Better not get ahead of ourselves and start at the beginning: what is assertive communication?

Assertive communication consists of expressing what you feel, think, want or need, without assaulting anyone, or feeling guilty for doing so. From a more technical point of view, it has been defined as "a communication that does not make any of the people involved in the interaction inferior, but emphasizes the accuracy of the communication and respect for all the people involved in the interaction" Duckworth, M.P; Mercer, V. (2 006).

Assertiveness is a great tool to make your relationships with others more equitable and at the same time you can express yourself freely. This is a social skill that you acquire with practice and that allows you to self-assert your rights, without letting yourself be manipulated or manipulated by anyone.

The purpose of assertive communication is to interact with others in an honest and direct way. Assertiveness is knowing how to ask, refuse or negotiate to achieve what you set out to do, always expressing your feelings in a clear way and respecting others. It also includes the ability to make and receive compliments, as well as the ability to make and receive complaints.

To help you fully understand the concept of assertive communication, it's worth briefly mentioning what communication styles are and why assertiveness is the best option.

Communication styles

When you communicate with others, and even if you don't realize it, you use a specific pattern. You may be very condescending, very taxing, or perhaps somewhat manipulative. This usually happens unconsciously. Based on typical patterns, four communication styles have been defined: passive, aggressive, passive-aggressive and assertive. Let's see what each of them is about.

Passive communication

It is the type of communication in which a person puts the interests and needs of others above their own. The goal is to please others, even if this makes you feel uncomfortable. It involves a lack of self-respect and a desire to avoid conflicts at all costs.

This type of communication usually leads to a person feeling misunderstood, ignored, and manipulated. Over time, this creates irritability, stress, and hostility. Likewise, their interlocutors may feel uncomfortable, since they have to "guess" what the passive person is thinking or feeling, because they don't say so. This may end up causing rejection.

Aggressive communication

Aggressive communication is the opposite position to the previous one. In this case, one's own interests and needs are placed above those of others. The objective is to impose itself on others, through hostile or threatening behaviors and gestures. It is possible for someone to initially achieve what they want, but they also expose themselves to counter-aggression or to experiencing feelings of guilt. Over time, this behavior creates distances and breaks.

Passive-aggressive communication

This type of communication is aggressive, but in an indirect or covert way. There are no shouts, insults or direct threats, but it also aims to impose itself on others. To do this, attitudes such as sarcasm, subtle disqualification, hostile silence, etc. In practice, the long-term effects are the same as those of aggressive communication: possible attacks, feelings of guilt, distance and rupture.

Assertive communication

As mentioned before, assertive communication is a style in which both one's own interests and needs and those of others are taken into account. It is based on mutual respect and three attitudes: being direct, being honest and being appropriate. It starts from a clear and sincere expression, without belittling anyone and takes into account the particular context of the other person. It fosters a healthy relationship with others and is a skill that develops: no one is born with it.

The importance of assertive communication in personal and professional life

Assertive communication is highly effective and functional. Using this style, you are much more likely to have your messages transmitted successfully. Passive, aggressive or passive-aggressive communication causes interference that limits mutual understanding.

Trying to please others is not only overwhelming, but it sends the message that what you think and feel isn't important. Therefore, others will end up ignoring you and this will create an internal conflict for you. In the same way, wanting to impose yourself on others will make your relationships tense and abusive. You will be involved in many conflicts and sooner rather than later you will generate rejection in others.

Communicating assertively, on the other hand, makes you freer. It gives rise to a large number of benefits, including the following:

1. **Reducing stress**. It helps you reduce tensions, both internally and with others.

2. **Increased self-esteem**. To the extent that you allow yourself to freely express what you think and feel, your self-love increases. Assertiveness is a form of self-affirmation.

3. **Increased self-confidence**. Respect for your own wants and needs strengthens trust in your own judgment.

4. **Increased sense of control**. Assertive communication helps you to rely less on other people's opinions and on the unconscious forces within you. You get more autonomy.

5. **Increase in self-knowledge**. Assertiveness requires you to be aware of your own emotions, thoughts and desires. Therefore, it helps you to know yourself better.

6. **Better management of emotions**. As your self-knowledge increases, you also understand yourself better and can channel your emotions more effectively.

7. **Reduce conflicts**. By having the ability to be clear and frank with others, but at the same time respect them, there is less chance of conflict.

8. **Better relationships with others**. Assertive communication promotes mutual respect and therefore helps build healthier relationships, both personally and professionally.

9. **Others**. The list would be endless, but among the most relevant benefits are the following: greater empowerment, more ability to manage solutions, better decision-making capacity, greater job satisfaction, etc.

What's stopping you?

At this point you may be wondering: if assertive communication is so good, then why are there so many who don't develop it? This is an excellent question and the answer gives us many clues for the work that we will develop in this book.

In general, there are four reasons why assertiveness is blocked. The first is the most obvious: assertive communication is not an innate skill, but an acquired one; this means that it does not happen to you spontaneously, but rather you have to work to develop it.

A second factor is education and upbringing. In some environments, inadequate communication is rewarded. For example, it is welcomed when a person gives up their rights to please others; this comes to be seen as an act of generosity. Likewise, in aggressive environments it is sometimes taught that the more intimidating someone is, the more likely they are to achieve success. Therefore, the person continues to use these communication styles, regardless of the damage they cause.

The third reason why people fail to communicate assertively is anxiety. If there is a lot of nervousness and ongoing distress, those emotions may take control and prevent someone from acting in a more rational and equanimous way.

Finally, many people do not act assertively because they do not know their rights and, therefore, do not defend them. In this regard, psychologist Manuel Smith, in his work When I Say No, I Feel Guilty (2003), points out that there are 10 basic assertive rights:

1. The right to be my own judge.

2. The right to choose whether to take responsibility for the problems of others.

3. The right to choose whether or not we want to give explanations.

4. The right to change your mind.

5. The right to make mistakes.

6. The right to say "I don't know".

7. The right not to need the approval of others.

8. The right to make decisions outside of logic.

9. The right not to understand the expectations of others.

10. The right not to try to achieve perfection.

What can this book bring you?

This book compiles the most up-to-date information on the subject, taking care that the source of the information has solid scientific and academic bases. The main objective is to provide you with concepts and tools that you can easily apply to different events in your personal and professional life. For this reason, we define it as a "friend book".

We will begin by dealing with one of the topics that arouses the most concerns, but which are usually talked about in a low voice: how to learn to say "no"? We will show you why it is an art and what is the way for you to know how to set limits and refuse to do everything that goes against your personal desire or need.

Then we'll move on to another crucial topic: how to talk without talking nonsense? In this section, we'll explain how to avoid empty speeches and how to increase two of the greatest communication skills: clarity and conciseness. Likewise, we are going to give you several relevant keys to developing a decisive competence: active listening.

Then we will delve into the world of persuasive communication. We will walk step by step through the labyrinths of the art of public speaking and we will give you essential tips so that not only are you not afraid to face large groups, but also to do so in the most efficient way possible.

To continue, we will address the topic of assertive communication within the framework of leadership. There you will find the keys to being an excellent leader, based on exercising authority in an assertive manner. We will also provide you with specific knowledge to know how and why to delegate functions, what is the way to resolve conflicts and how you can motivate a work team.

We will finish by talking about one of the essential axes: self-esteem. In this final section, you will find valuable principles and strategies to increase self-love and overcome obstacles that prevent you from having more confidence in yourself. You'll love this section.

You'll find a series of exercises at the end of each chapter. The objective is that they become functional tools to put into practice what has been learned. You should be aware that the more you apply the knowledge we are going to give you, the greater the chances of achieving healthier communication and, with it, a fuller life.

Are you ready to start this journey to a better life? If the answer is "yes" all that remains is to turn to this page and accept the challenge of starting an adventure towards your well-being.

CHAPTER 1: LEARN TO SAY "NO" IN STYLE

"Because no one can know for you. No one can grow for you. No one can search for you. No one can do for you what you must do yourself. Existence does not admit representatives". -Jorge Bucay-

It is possible that World War II would have been avoided, if the Europeans had said "no" to Hitler when they were in time to do so. France and the USSR had agreements to defend Czechoslovakia if it was attacked by another nation. The Germans, governed by the Nazi party, had obvious intentions to invade that country, and other nations knew that.

However, instead of joining together to reject these pretensions, what they did was meet with the Führer and accept that he should keep much of the Czechoslovak territory. A year later, Hitler not only had that nation under his command, but practically all of Europe. In the end, that bloody war cost the lives of more than 50 million people.

These real events show us the importance of saying "no" in time. Some believe that being condescending is the best way to keep things peaceful, but as we have seen, sometimes it only serves to pave the way for much greater conflict. The same thing happens in personal life.

In this chapter we will talk about the importance of knowing how to say "no" in the right way. We will see why it is so difficult for some people to do so and what are the reasons why it is necessary to develop this skill. We will also give you several practical tips to avoid feelings of guilt and deal with the negative reactions of the interlocutor. Finally, we are going to propose some exercises for you to practice and develop this skill.

1.1 The importance of setting limits

"Daring to set limits is about having the courage to love ourselves, even when we risk disappointing others." -Brene and Brown-

Setting limits doesn't mean rejecting others or defending your opinion or beliefs hard and hard. Rather, it has to do with letting others know what you need and what you don't, what you want and what you don't. In other words, define the frontier of what is acceptable and desirable for you, and what is not.

In the framework of assertive communication, you don't have to go over anyone to assert yourself. You just need to make it clear what you expect, want and allow. You can send that message in an empathetic and friendly way, so that the other person doesn't feel offended or rejected.

Why is it important to set limits?

To understand the importance of setting boundaries, think for a moment about your home. Imagine that anyone can enter there, at any time and without restrictions. If they want, they also have the right to use your belongings, eat what's in your fridge, use your toothbrush, etc. How would you feel? Surely, you would stop thinking that this is your home and you would begin to perceive it as a public place.

Exactly the same thing happens when you don't set limits on dealing with others. Many people will feel entitled to use and abuse your time, your patience, your generosity and who knows how many other things. You become more of an object than a subject.

The consequences of this are unpredictable. You may be exposed to a number of abuses and you may have to deal with the most toxic side of many people. Your personal evolution will stagnate and you will feel more and more ignored. This may lead you to incubate resentments, resentments, anger, and frustration. It's not an enviable situation.

The Benefits of Setting Boundaries

Setting boundaries is the best way to preserve your identity and personal well-being. It offers many benefits, but there are four that are especially important: self-knowledge, self-esteem, respect for yourself and balanced relationships with others.

Setting limits is a way to get in touch with yourself. It means becoming aware of what you want and need. Knowing or discovering what is pleasant or tolerable for you involves an exercise in self-knowledge. Perhaps without realizing it, you consult with yourself and you are defining what are the borders that others should not cross.

Reaffirming your identity in front of others increases your appreciation for yourself. In fact, it is an expression of self-respect and self-care. You may not notice it, but people end up treating you, just like you treat yourself. Therefore, setting limits is an action and a process that leads to others also appreciating and respecting you more.

The biggest prize: freedom

The biggest prize you get for setting limits is freedom. It seems contradictory, but it is not. If you give yourself the place you deserve in interactions with others, you will lose your fear of showing yourself as you are. You'll feel free to express yourself, regardless of whether or not others approve of who you are.

When a person feels very vulnerable in front of others, they flee or attack. In both cases, he does it to defend himself, because he feels weak and maintains constant tension. It's the fear of being harmed or hurt. For this reason, it cannot express itself spontaneously and relates to the world in an artificial way.

On the other hand, when someone is confident in their ability to set limits, they feel liberated. He knows that he has the power to prevent harm that others want to inflict on him. He also understands that he doesn't have to confront, or walk over, someone to get respect for him.

Do you want an example?

Let's think about an everyday situation.

By accident, someone trips over a glass of soda and spills it. Another person who sees him says: "What a fool!" The person who committed the minor offense may blush and ask for forgiveness; they may also respond aggressively: "Is there a problem?"

Or, perhaps, he'll show off his ability to set limits and say something like this: "Do you really think I'm a fool because I had this little accident?"

The last one is an answer that invites us to reflect on the validity of the statement. At the same time, implicitly, it sets a limit that could be expressed as follows: "It is not you who qualifies my actions. I have my own judgment in judging what I do."

Why do some people fail to set limits?

Most commonly, people refrain from setting limits out of fear of rejection. In short, people are more harmless when you let them do what they want with you. If you express yourself and say "so far" they probably don't feel comfortable.

Another factor that influences is the feeling of guilt. You've gotten so used to letting others override your wants and needs that you feel strange if you don't allow it. In addition, you may be convinced that this attitude is proof of your nobility and good character. That is why you experience reaffirmation as a selfish and unvirtuous behavior.

Insecurity, fear of confrontation, lack of self-esteem or lack of communication skills are other factors that can lead you to not set limits when it is necessary to do so. The question is: how do you learn to set limits, without this becoming a conflict for you? A good starting point is to learn to say "no" in an appropriate way. We'll talk about this below.

1.2 How to say "NO" assertively

"Let's say what we have to say. We can say it softly, but firmly, speaking from the heart. We don't need to be critical or tactless, or blame or be cruel when we tell our truths." -Melody Beattie-

Saying "no" is a skill that requires training, especially if you have a hard time doing so. It is very convenient to say "yes" to situations that, even if they cause you discomfort, also bring you something. Like when a colleague invites you to watch a movie and you're a little tired, but it's a film that interests you and you also tend to enjoy the company of the person who invites you.

On the other hand, if the film seems like a mess to you and your partner is a heavy one, but you want to look good with him because after all there is a close relationship, you're in trouble. These are the cases in which it is very important to know how to say "no". To put it more specifically: you should never do something just to please another person, especially if that means stepping over yourself.

However, this does not mean that you have the right to completely ignore what the other person feels, thinks or expects of you. The purpose of saying "no" is to respect your own wishes and needs, but without disrespecting those of the other. In the example we are talking about, if you say "no" there is a rejection, but it doesn't have to be brutal or inconsiderate.

Assertive techniques for saying "no"

When there is a situation in which your needs and desires conflict with the needs and desires of another person, it is best for you to choose what is best for you. Of course, this involves putting others in the background. How to do it without causing harm? There are some techniques that help to achieve this. The most commonly used are the following.

The sandwich technique

The sandwich technique consists of expressing a positive message before and after rejection. The goal is to soften rejection and leave a sense of empathy in the other person. For example: "It's very nice of you to invite me, but I can't accept because I'm tired. I hope there is another lucky person who does accept your invitation."

The scratched disc

The broken disc technique should only be used when someone is very insistent. You've already told him no, but he's determined to change your mind. If so, it is best to repeat the same answer, without variations, as many times as the other one insists. "I can't accept your invitation"... "I can't accept your invitation"... "I can't accept your invitation"...

The fog bank

This technique consists of camouflaging rejection within the context of the message. In this way, a partial agreement is expressed with the other, even if in essence there is a refusal. It is used when it is foreseeable that the other person will take the rejection the wrong way. For example: "I can't wait to see that movie, but I can't accept your invitation because I have other plans."

Explain the consequences

This technique is applied by explaining in detail and with serenity the possible consequences of saying "yes". For example, "I can't accept your invitation because I'm so tired and I'm probably going to fall asleep watching the movie, which would be a waste." It is used when the other person is highly susceptible to rejection.

The three-part phrase

This technique is similar to the sandwich technique, but in this case a positive phrase is used before rejection, the manifestation of rejection and, finally, what you want to see happen. For example: "Your invitation is great and I thank you, but I can't accept it because I'm exhausted and I prefer to go and rest."

What's stopping you from saying "no"?

If you are a person who is used to saying "yes", it will most likely take some time to learn to say "no". Remember that this requires training. Before you practice, it might be a good idea to explore a little bit about the reasons why you have trouble refusing someone else's requests.

Some do not know or are not convinced that refusing something is a right. It is defined as a right because it refers to the power that every human being has to reject what is inconvenient or inappropriate for them. A person must first look after himself in order to be able to look after others.

On the other hand, you most likely have the wrong idea about what a refusal means. When you say "no", what you are refusing is the request and not the person making it to you. That's why it's so important to refuse in an appropriate way. That is, making the other person feel that your goal is to reaffirm your desire or need, and not to underestimate or disqualify what he or she needs or wants.

Likewise, you may not have noticed that saying "yes" to all the demands or demands of others means saying "no" to your own interests. So the question is: who is more important: you or the other? If you don't have an immediate answer to this question, perhaps your problem is that refusing someone else's requirements causes you guilt.

1.3 How to avoid feeling guilty in 5 quick and painless steps

"If we are very careful not to hurt anyone under any circumstances, we will end up hurting ourselves and others." -P. Jakubowski-

Many people think that prioritizing themselves is a sign of selfishness. Therefore, they are unable to refuse someone else's request. They assume that they will be morally disapproved and that is why they experience feelings of guilt when they give more importance to "me" than to "you".

If you have traveled on an airplane, you will remember that, before taking off, the flight attendants give a series of instructions on how to act in case of emergency. One of them points out that, if it is necessary to wear an oxygen mask, it must first be put on by the passenger and only then should it help others to put it on. Why? Because someone without air doesn't make it easier for others to breathe. This is also how life works.

As you can see, at no time is there talk of taking care only of oneself, but of doing so before pretending to take care of others. Misunderstood solidarity is what leads to feelings of guilt. Meeting the needs of others, overcoming oneself, in the long run only leads to internal discomfort that ends up poisoning relationships with others.

5 keys to not feeling guilty

The first reason you shouldn't feel guilty when you say "no" is that you have the right to do so. Do you think that others have an obligation to say "yes" to everything you ask of them? Of course not. All people have the right to protect our internal world from experiences that go against what we think or feel. There is nothing wrong with that. On the contrary, it is the healthiest thing and could even be classified as a duty to oneself.

Next, we give you five keys to avoid feelings of guilt when you don't please others.

1. **You can't please everyone**. No matter what you do, there will always be someone who questions your behavior. Even Mother Teresa of Calcutta has detractors. Therefore, you must banish the idea that you are in the world to please everyone around you and try to keep them satisfied. If you do, for sure, you will be harmed.

2. **Anxiety is part of the process**. It's clear that when you say "no" to someone, it creates tension with that person. It is normal that this is the case. You may experience some anxiety or distress when you see the other person's reaction and this may turn into a feeling of guilt. You shouldn't give in just to stop feeling that discomfort. If you practice "no" frequently, little by little you will feel less discomfort.

3. **Do you have enough energy to say "yes"?** No human being has enough strength to carry on the problems of others indefinitely, without something breaking inside them. The healthy thing is to set priorities and offer your help only when you are in a position to do so. It should be a free decision and one that does not cause you discomfort.

4. **Rationalize the situation** One key to avoiding feelings of guilt is to rationalize the situation. How to do it? Just think about the real consequences of saying "no" to a person. Do you leave her in a situation of extreme helplessness or need? Is there no other human being who can fulfill your requirement? Is saying "yes" going to radically change your situation? Also, examine your own reasons for saying "yes" or "no". Would you say "yes" just to avoid conflict? Would you do it just because you don't want to upset or make the other person feel bad? What feeling would be present inside you after doing something you don't want to? Respond with your hand on your heart.

5. **Think about your values and priorities** If you are clear about your values and priorities, it will be much easier for you to refuse to do something that goes against what you believe in. Now, solidarity is very likely to top your list, but don't forget that first of all you must be in solidarity with yourself. From this, you can define the rest. If you act in accordance with your principles, you don't have to experience feelings of guilt.

How to handle the situation?

It's important to be very attentive to what you feel when someone asks you for a favor or asks you for something that doesn't benefit you. If you experience stress, discouragement or tiredness, it means that you don't have the emotional availability to respond to that person's request. The healthy thing is to have respect for what you feel and to deny yourself. If, on the other hand, there is no reticence or it is very low, you could well accept.

If you're not sure what you want to answer, it's best to take a few minutes to think about the situation. Evaluate if you have the willingness, time and capacity to do what they ask of you. If they demand an immediate response, apply assertive communication: "I can't give you an immediate answer. I need to think for a moment to know what to do."

The best thing is to always give a direct and honest answer in the end, without ambiguity. Avoid softening the "no" by saying that maybe in the future you will do what they ask of you or giving explanations that are not being asked of you. Part of the process of being assertive has to do with learning to be frank, with serenity and courtesy.

It could be very enriching to make a list of all those situations in which you experience strong feelings of guilt when you say "no". Examine them carefully and try to analyze why you feel guilty and exactly where the supposed mistake you make in refusing is. This self-knowledge exercise is usually very useful to better understand yourself.

1.4 Learning to deal with negativity and people's reactions

"If it is a duty to respect the rights of others, so is it to defend one's own."

-Herbert Spencer-

The experiments of Solomon Asch (1950) are a classic in contemporary psychology. These researchers thoroughly studied the subject of social pressure and compliance. In one of the first studies they conducted, they asked a group of students about the length of two lines drawn on paper: which was shorter and which was longer?

The truth is that all the students, except one, agreed with the researchers to give the wrong answers. The person who was unaware of the agreement was confused to see that most people said that the shortest line was the longest and vice versa. The experiment was repeated many times. In the end, in 36% of the cases, the student who ignored the experiment ended up agreeing with the majority, even though the error was evident. Why did they do it? Peer pressure was decisive. It made them afraid to depart from the general opinion.

These experiments give us an idea of how overwhelming the effect of the opinion of others can be on our perceptions and beliefs. It also gives an idea of the consequences of worrying excessively about what others think. In fact, there is a phobia known as the "Taijin Kyofusho Disorder" which consists of an extreme fear of offending others. It is born of insecurity and an almost delirious obsession with showing oneself to others as someone "perfect".

Without going to those extreme cases, the truth is that saying "no" to someone causes frustration in the other. Some will respond in a reasonable manner, respecting the refusal. Others, on the other hand, will assume a hostile attitude and will even want to make you feel guilty. How to get around this? Let's see.

The reaction of others

The world is full of manipulative people who react excessively when others don't please them. It is very common for these to be individuals who make victimize their flag. They are always in trouble, or have some shortcomings, and that is why they expect others to compensate them. That's why they feel entitled to reproach when someone doesn't give in to their requirements.

There are also those who in the past have done something for you and believe that precedent is a Corsican patent to demand that you correspond. If you don't give in to their demands, they have no problem getting rid of the supposed emotional or material debts you have with them in your face.

Likewise, emotional blackmail is likely to be used in this type of situation. It happens when the other person tells you that, if you really care for her or him, you should say "yes" to everything. It could also point out to you that your refusal is evidence of a lack of understanding or support.

In these cases, the reaction is an act of frank manipulation. In principle, the reasons they use may sound very reasonable, but if you analyze them thoroughly, you realize that it is a psychological game with the sole purpose of putting yourself at their service. The more manipulative a person is, the more intense their reaction to a refusal will be. Don't forget that.

The fear of conflict

The main reason why many abstain from saying "no" is fear of conflict. They feel that disagreements cause a lot of tension and that they don't have the psychological tools to tolerate this discomfort. For this reason, a priori they say "yes" to everything, in order to avoid that bitter drink.

In this regard, it must be said that conflict is as normal as blinking. For this reason, it should not be seen as a negative reality, but rather it is consubstantial to life in society. Distant, artificial or false relationships are the only ones that do not generate disagreements or tensions. In real relationships, it is impossible for there to be consensus all the time. Or that emotions are so balanced that all tension is eliminated.

So, the conflict will exist, whether you seek it or not. The real problem is not in the presence of the conflict, but in the way it is managed. Discomfort does not stem from difference of opinion, but rather from reactions to it. Let's see.

The aggressive reaction

Reacting aggressively to a conflict only makes it intensify or multiply. If someone imposes himself on another, as a means of settling differences, it will not only lead to the conflict remaining intact, but silenced, but it will also give rise to hostilities that will sooner or later manifest. Therefore, being aggressive is not at all effective.

The passive reaction

Avoiding conflicts has the same effect as accepting them aggressively. Ultimately, nothing is resolved, but rather is concealed or silenced, while the contradiction persists. Therefore, evasive or passive attitudes can only prolong a problem that could well be solved using the appropriate strategy.

Conflict is positive!

Although a conflict involves a dose of tension and anxiety, the truth is that, if properly managed, it becomes a positive element. Why? Because it constitutes an opportunity to bring about constructive change and helps the people involved to mature.

It's not healthy to allow disagreements or disagreements to continue. No problem goes away or diminishes just by ignoring it. On the contrary, difficulties that are not addressed in time tend to become increasingly profound and complex. Conflict is an episode in which these contradictions come to the surface and that is why the most intelligent thing is to see it as the right opportunity to resolve what is wrong. We will come back to this topic later.

10 practical tips for dealing with the reaction of others

If you want to say "no" but don't know how to deal with the other person's hostile or guilty reaction, take note of the following tips.

- **One: Give credit to your own judgment**

If the other person judges your behavior and rates it in a negative way, remember that what matters most are your reasons for acting the way you do. You're trying to preserve your well-being, because you have the right to it. You want to be true to your own emotions, principles and values. So the best thing is not to give more credit to what the other person thinks of you. There is an old maxim: "Don't judge my path if you haven't been in my shoes".

- **Two: The difficulty is with the other person, not with you**

If the other person doesn't want to listen to or understand your reasons, it's best to look for a way to express yourself more clearly. If he still maintains his position and locks in on his own arguments, you must assume that the difficulty is with that person and not with you.

- **Three: Approach the situation in a constructive way**

As we have already warned before, conflict is positive if it is handled in an intelligent way. The rejection or hostile attitude of the other person can also be the starting point for addressing the underlying problem and reaching an agreement.

It is an opportunity to, for example, ask: "Why do you think I should answer yes, when I don't want to?" If you don't find receptivity in the other person, however, these types of situations help you to learn more about the other person and to practice assertive communication.

- **Four: Focus on what you want to do**

The other person's reaction could lead you to lose focus on the situation. You may end up giving explanations about your rights and objectives, when this is not necessary. Therefore, the best thing is to emphasize that you are doing what you want. You do this because you have the right and duty to look after yourself. There is no need to add anything else.

- **Five: Don't let them undermine your self-esteem**

Sometimes the other person will try to disqualify or downplay you when you refuse to do anything they want. Don't allow it. In fact, it's very important that you make efforts to work on your self-esteem all the time. Such a situation is ideal for testing yourself. If you manage to maintain the respect you have for yourself, you will also be nourishing your self-love.

- **Six: Be aware of the need for approval**

If you have a strong need to be approved by others, it's important to be aware of this. Why is this happening? Examine in particular the upbringing you received or the messages they have given you regarding the importance of pleasing others. Think about whether they instilled in you the idea that refusing someone's requests is a way to lose their affection or to generate rejection. If so, take a cold look at whether it is reasonable for this to happen.

- **Seven: Delimit the scope of rejection**

If the other person rejects your attitude, remember that they are only rejecting that behavior and not you as a human being. In the same way, you must make him understand that you are refusing his request, not that person as such. The refusal of that person does not make you any more or less valuable, and your refusal should not be seen as a total closure to any other request they make to you.

- **Eight: Remember that you can't please everyone**

You didn't come into the world to please all people. Some will feel very enriched by what you can bring to them. Others will not value what you are. This is normal, so stop thinking that only if everyone approves of you, are you right. Even the Saints have critics.

- **Nine: Only you own your emotions**

If another person says something aggressive to you, only you decide if you accept that emotion or not. You can take it very seriously, or rather understand that that person is responding inadequately to something they don't like. At the same time, it is he or she who must deal with their negative emotion and that you should only limit yourself to not letting yourself be infected by that inappropriate feeling.

- **Ten: Evaluate your perfectionist beliefs**

If you have a very severe self-demand, you are going to resent very intensely any criticism they make of you. That's why it's important that you reevaluate your attitude. Think about whether it's reasonable to have such high expectations. Is it good for you or does it limit you? Does it promote your evolution or does it frequently cause you emotional discomfort?

1.5 Exercises to improve the ability to say NO

Assertive communication is a skill that is learned in practice. You can read 100 volumes on the subject, but if you don't apply the basic principles in your daily interactions, so much information will be of no use to you.

To begin with, we invite you to perform some exercises and tasks that will help you strengthen your ability to be assertive and, in particular, to learn to say "no", without feeling guilty or hurting other people.

The Fatal Inventory

Take a pen and paper to make a list of 10 times you remember saying "yes" when you really wanted to say "no". Choose the most prominent ones throughout your life and think about the consequences that resulted from your affirmative answer.

Wishlist

You should also make a list, but in this case the goal is to identify all those everyday situations in which you would like to stop saying "yes" just to please others. Imagine how you would feel when you refused.

Dissection

Take one of the situations you described in exercises 1 and 2. Describe how the situation developed. What happened in the beginning? What was the other person's attitude when making the request? What did you feel at the time? Why did you say "yes"? What was the other person's response or attitude when you signed in? What did you feel after this episode and how do you remember it?

Identify your pattern

Try to specify as precisely as possible the chain of emotions that occurs in you when someone asks you for something and you agree to this, against your desire. Define each emotion with a word. Does it always happen the same way? If not, could you identify another or other chains of emotions?

Imagine problem situations

To do this exercise, you must imagine situations in which a person you appreciate or fear makes you a request that you do not want to accept. Next, think about how you would apply the techniques to say "no": the sandwich technique, the fog bank, explaining the consequences, the three-part phrase and the scratched disc.

The top 5 responsibilities

Identify five of the responsibilities that you frequently assume, without being clear about why they are being assigned to you. Think about the reason why others think that it is you who should bear that burden and why you think that should not be the case.

Identify critical situations

Think about who are the people you find it most difficult to say "no" with. Also, what are the requests that are the most difficult for you to refuse. Try to pinpoint why this is happening. In principle, this will help you be more alert with those specific people and in those particular situations.

Practice "no"

Start with situations where your refusal isn't as compromising. It's a good idea to go to a supermarket and when you get to the checkout, tell the person in charge that you've thought better and you don't want to carry that product anymore. Say that "no" as strongly as possible and think about how you feel. You can then practice it several times in similar situations. You're going to realize that it wasn't as difficult as you thought.

Meditate

Find a place where you can be alone and uninterrupted. Ideally, it should be a comfortable place. Sit down and start taking a deep breath. Try to follow the path of the air with your mind, from the moment you take it through your nose and through your respiratory system, to your lungs. Then, back, from your lungs until it comes out through your mouth. Repeat for five continuous minutes, every day, for a week. It will help you connect with yourself.

Search for a cause

It would be very useful for you to join a cause, either for the defense of the environment, a political party or any topic that matches what you believe in. He works for that cause at least a couple of hours a week. This will help you to assert yourself as an individual.

Conclusion

Knowing how to say "no" is one of the most important assertive skills. It is a necessary tool to preserve your well-being and reaffirm your identity in all kinds of circumstances. Likewise, it is one of the factors that will allow you to empower yourself and, in this way, take charge of your own destiny.

Based on what is seen in this chapter, keep in mind the following premises:

- Knowing how to set limits on others gives you greater freedom to be who you are, without others conditioning your behavior.

- There are several assertive techniques for saying "no". Some of them are the sandwich, the scratched disc, the fog bank, explaining the consequences and the three-part phrase.

- The feeling of guilt is one of the main factors why a person is unable to say "no" when they want to do so.

- The best way to avoid feeling guilty about saying "no" is to accept that you are entitled to it and that it is impossible to please everyone. The best thing to do is to rationalize the situation and stick to one's own values and principles.

- The best way to say "no" is to do it directly and honestly, without blunts or ambiguities.

- You need to be prepared to deal with someone's negative reactions when you say "no" to them. The most important thing is to understand that these types of conflicts can be very constructive, if handled in the right way.

In the next chapter we are going to address one of the most important topics in assertive communication: clarity and concreteness. We will answer questions such as: How to speak to make you understand? How to talk less and say more? What are the keys to making your messages more effective and persuasive? What is it and how can you develop the ability to listen actively? What is all this good for you? We are waiting for you!

CHAPTER 2: TALK WITHOUT TALKING NONSENSE

"Take care of your thoughts, because they will become your words. Watch your words, because they will become your actions. Take care of your actions, because they will become your habits. Take care of your habits, because they will become your destiny" -Gandhi-

Do you know where the expression "speaking through the elbows" comes from?

Everything indicates that it refers to the fact that those who talk a lot only get their interlocutor distracted frequently. Therefore, they have to touch his elbow repeatedly, to get them to pay attention to them again. This is precisely what is achieved when you talk a lot and say little: that others stop paying attention to what you say.

It is estimated that currently a person receives between 3,000 and 5,000 advertising messages per day. Likewise, it is believed that the average person is exposed to about 30 gigabytes of information daily. This is equivalent to something like 10,000 normal-sized books. All this has led to a new pathology: intoxication.

We talk about everything and receive information every second, but we can't process most of the data that comes to us. All of the above is enough reason to worry about reducing the amount of information that is transmitted and received on a daily basis, increasing quality at the same time. How to do it? That's what we'll talk about in this chapter.

2.1 How to avoid empty speeches

"Words are like coins, because one is worth many as many are not worth one." -Francisco de Quevedo-

An empty discourse is one in which there is a high flow of words, but, at the same time, a low transmission of concepts. In other words, talk a lot and say little. It is not always easy to detect it, because it is often hidden behind bombastic or very striking rhetoric.

Empty speeches are characterized by their lack of substance. They are full of clichés and generalities. There is a continuous repetition of words or ideas, as well as many explanations for what is obvious. Sometimes, the lack of content is camouflaged behind complex words or apparently profound disquisitions, which no one understands. In these cases, when you look in detail, you don't find solid or interesting ideas behind this tangle of complexity either.

Language is the envelope of thought. Therefore, we could say that an empty discourse represents an absence of ideas. The problem is that this lack is easily disguised and that is how many end up paying attention to what does not deserve it.

The characteristics of empty speech

Empty speech has some traits that make it identifiable. How can you recognize it? The main characteristics of this type of communication are the following.

Many words, few ideas

This is the most characteristic feature of empty speech. He says in 20 words what he could say in five. There is no intention of communicating specific ideas or concepts, but rather it focuses on an endless discussion that often does not know where it is going.

Never-ending repetition

Another characteristic of empty speech is the fact that many repetitions are made in it, without need. The same idea is expressed in different ways, even if it is something very simple. This trait can also be seen in the repetition of words.

Lots of rodeos

In empty discourse, a lot of blunts are made around a simple approach. It's like you can't get to the point once and for all. This is because, in reality, there is no essence to reach.

Dispersion

In this type of speech we talk about everything and nothing at the same time. There is no order in the approach of ideas and that is why, often, the topic ends up drifting to issues that have nothing to do with the initial or central issue.

Rhetoric

This is one of the most deceptive features of some empty speeches. The speaker is very fluent and easy to speak. It uses a large number of adjectives and usually offers impressive phrases. That's why it can even be nice to listen to it, even if in the end it's not saying anything.

Avoid empty speech

In a world full of information, it's not worth talking for the sake of talking. Unfortunately, hardly anyone understands this. There is a belief that the more a person talks, the more active their mind is. However, speaking too well is usually a sign of anxiety or insecurity.

How to avoid that tendency to talk without saying anything? Take note of the following tips.

Think before you speak

Even in casual conversations, it's always important to think before you speak. You don't have to make a detailed plan, but you do need to avoid impulsiveness. Take it easy, pause, and then express yourself. This is even more important in situations that are tense or involve important issues.

Learn to listen

Listening is as important as saying. If you're in an everyday conversation, pay attention to what the other person is saying to you. Don't interrupt her before she finishes speaking. Listen not only to their words, but also to their attitude: that is also a form of listening.

Get to the point

Try to focus on a single topic and delve deeper into it, before moving on to another topic. Blunting and rambling only disperse your message and eventually make it more confusing. It's good to complement the core idea, illustrate it, bring up examples, and use resources to reinforce your point. What's not good is to beat around the bush and get lost in a jungle of words.

The good thing, if brief...

There is a famous aphorism by Baltasar Gracián that says: "The good, if brief, twice good". There couldn't be wiser advice. To express more ideas with fewer words is to achieve excellence in communication. Give each idea just the right number of words and don't dwell on what doesn't merit it.

Prioritize descriptions

It is always better to describe than to qualify so as not to fall into empty discourse. When making a description, you force yourself to specify the ideas; on the other hand, if you focus on the qualification, you will only be transmitting a subjective perception. You are more concrete and clear when you say "The sky is blue and cloudless" than when you point out "The sky is transparent and smooth". Do you notice the difference?

Raise your language skills

One of the keys to avoiding empty speeches is to improve your ability to express yourself. The more you know the language and the more skills you develop, the better your oral and written communication will be. The ideal way to increase your language ability is reading. Without realizing it, this enriches your speech and also provides you with quality information that you can then share.

2.2 The importance of being clear and concise in communication

"A strong voice cannot compete with a clear voice, even if it is a simple murmur." -Confucius-

One of the most important aspects of communication is making sure that the message reaches the receiver in the most appropriate way. If the interlocutor does not understand what you say to him, has difficulty following the thread of your thinking or loses interest in what you say, the communication process is interrupted and runs the risk of breaking down.

The factor that most disrupts good communication is lack of clarity. The philosopher Ludwig Wittgenstein said the following phrase in the foreword to his work Tractatus logico-philosophicus: "What can even be said can be said clearly; and what cannot be talked about must be kept silent". What did he mean? In short, you should only talk when you are clear about the idea to be expressed. And that everything must be said simply.

One of the elements that most favors clarity is conciseness. The Royal Spanish Academy (RAE) defines it as "Brevity and economy of media in the way of expressing a concept with accuracy". In other words: use as few words as possible to say something and be precise.

Thus, clarity and conciseness are the two main axes of an effective message. Let's look at each of these concepts in greater detail.

Clarity

Communicating clearly is a skill that includes several variables. The first of these are words. It's always best to choose the terms that are most understandable. Using strange or very technical words, even with a specialized audience, tends to alter communication.

The second element has to do with the way you organize words into phrases and sentences. The simplest constructions are also the most understandable and effective. Instead of saying "It's not true that that person didn't want to attend", better point out "That person wanted to attend". The meaning is the same, but obviously in the second case it is easier to understand it.

A third aspect has to do with coherence. Your speech becomes much clearer when it follows a logical order. Let's say you want to talk about gifted people. The most reasonable thing would be to start by saying what they are, what their characteristics are, how their abilities manifest, etc. If you start by talking about the adaptation problems of the gifted, without having mentioned who they are and what characterizes them, your interlocutor is likely to be confused and unable to follow your presentation of ideas. The same thing happens when you run into contradictions. Coherence is a key element of clarity and vice versa.

Conciseness

The clarity of the expression depends largely on conciseness. The way to be concise is to become very stingy with words. Don't waste them. Use just the right number of terms to say something. Also, dose the information you're providing: don't try to cram five ideas into a single sentence.

One of the aspects you should look at is the subject of repetition. If you've already said something, you don't have to repeat it, unless your conscious goal is to reinforce and fix this message. It also eliminates crutches.

Enriching your lexicon is very positive to be more concise and clear. Try to avoid words with vague meanings such as "bad", "good", "good", "bad", etc. If you try a little, you will surely find much more precise synonyms. By the way, they'll save you a lot of words.

Of course, it is very important to eliminate data that is irrelevant, obvious or does not provide information. So are the rodeos: it's always better to go straight to the subject. Failing to do so is distracting and can even become a little nerve-racking. Being laconic is also not an appropriate option. The ideal is to seek a balance in the use of words: not so many that overwhelm your interlocutor, nor so few that you leave him on the rocks.

2.3 The Master Plan for communicating clearly and concisely

"Between two explanations, choose the clearest; between two forms, the simplest; between two expressions, the shortest". -Eugene d'Ors-

We are all capable of communicating in a clear and concise way, under any circumstances. Some people have a natural ability to use language fluently and almost seamlessly. Others, on the other hand, are not as skilled at handling speech or writing. However, whatever the case, there is always room for improvement.

Problems of clarity and conciseness usually have two origins: either it is necessary to develop some language skills, or it is an emotional problem that can also be worked on. In the latter case, excessive shyness, anxiety or psychological rigidity play tricks on the table.

Anyway, there are several techniques that can help you raise your level of communication. The most important thing is not that you know them, but that you practice them. They are all very simple and you just need a little perseverance for them to take effect. Let's see what they are.

1- Make a mind map or a basic outline

As we have already indicated before, it is always good to think before speaking. However, in intimate or casual conversations there is much wider scope for spontaneity. Instead, a professional or academic situation requires much more control of the situation. In such cases, stating your ideas in a clear and concise way becomes a critical factor.

Therefore, it is best to draw up an outline or a mental map before speaking. If this is a short or not very formal intervention, all you have to do is write down the central idea on a piece of paper and perhaps one or two secondary ideas. Do it in order from highest to lowest importance. This helps you stay focused and keeps you in order.

If your intervention is longer, especially if it is of special importance (as is the case, for example, in a trial), it is best to draw up a mental map. It defines the central idea and five secondary ideas, each in a single sentence. If this is the case, also write down the tertiary ideas or indicate the elements that complement the secondary ideas. Make a graph in which all this is captured, in a hierarchical way, as if it were an organization chart.

2- Define a goal

To maintain the coherence of your speech and avoid going around the bush, the best thing to do is to clearly define what the purpose of communication is. What are you looking for when you speak? Should the other person or group convince themselves that something is positive or negative? Or, rather, do you intend to motivate them? Or, perhaps, to question an idea?

If you have a clear objective, it will be much easier for you to direct your words towards that purpose.

3- Think about your interlocutor

The more you know your interlocutor, the more likely you are to achieve effective communication. For purposes of clarity, you should take into account the average level of knowledge, as well as the interests of the other person. Addressing a child is not the same as addressing an adult; just as speaking to your boss is not the same as talking to a co-worker.

In general, you should not use strange references or unusual technicalities, even if you are talking to a specialized interlocutor. If it is necessary to use words of little use or little-known references, you should give a brief explanation. Don't assume that the other person has certain knowledge.

4- Take into account the context

Context becomes another determining factor in communication. If you do your intervention in an environment dominated by conflict, your words will have a different effect than if you do so within the framework of a situation in which there is harmony.

The main elements to consider are the emotional climate, the availability of time, the good or bad attitude of your interlocutor, the comfort of the space, interruptions, etc. Sometimes a good conversation is interrupted or altered by factors that don't seem important to the naked eye, such as heavy rain or a lot of heat. Take all of these elements into account when speaking.

5- Define a strategy

If the conversation or intervention is very important, the best thing is to define a communication strategy. This is an expansion of the mind map. You must be very clear about what you are going to say first and what comes after. It is also important to establish whether it is necessary to use help, such as examples or graphics, to make it easier to understand some complex aspects.

Strategy refers to the "how" you are going to convey your message, based on your objectives, the interlocutor and the context, with an emphasis on clarity and conciseness. You must answer the following questions: What are the most difficult aspects of your message to understand? Why? How could they be more understandable? What elements can cause confusion? Do they need to be maintained? If so, how can you make them clear to others?

6- Take care of your non-verbal language

Remember that nonverbal language communicates more than verbal language. Your postures and gestures can significantly help clarify a message. The tone of your voice and your attitude will tell others if you are dealing with a very serious matter or if you are dealing with something that is not very important.

Your non-verbal language unconsciously contributes to creating an emotional climate during the conversation or intervention. It reinforces what you say or it may contradict it. If you don't manage this variable well, the best thing is to try to adopt neutral postures and gestures, so that you don't generate "noise" in communication.

7- Reduce the speed of speech

The pace of speaking is another factor that influences the clarity of your message. As a general rule, you don't want to express your words at high speed. First of all, it's going to be difficult to follow you, especially if you're talking about something that isn't easy to understand. Secondly, you impart restlessness and even nervousness in your interlocutor.

One of the effects of nervousness is to cause rapid speech. If this happens to you, just take a short break and try to breathe more slowly. If you speak with less speed, your words will naturally take on an authoritative tone and you will get your interlocutors to pay more attention. You'll also better control the flow of your thinking.

8- Project your voice well

Although it usually seems like a minor factor, the truth is that if you speak too quietly they won't listen to you and, at the same time, this could affect the understanding of the message. If you breathe properly, your voice will project much better.

It is common for shyness to lead to speaking at a low volume. It's as if a person is ashamed of what they have to say. In addition to sending an inappropriate message about yourself, it also interferes with clarity. It's important to practice so that your voice is properly projected.

9- Pronounce words correctly

Clarity also includes the correct pronunciation of each word. In fact, if you pronounce correctly, without realizing it, you'll just be more focused on what you're saying, you'll slow down and project your voice better.

10- Less is more

This is the golden premise of good communication. Whenever you can eliminate ideas that don't bring much, or words with little meaning, do so. Being synthetic is an acquired skill that is achieved with daily practice.

2.4 Do you already know your negative thoughts and cognitive distortions?

"Few things in the world are as powerful as positivity. A smile. A word of optimism and hope. You can do it when things go wrong." -Richard DeVos-

Until now, we have focused on the importance of avoiding empty speeches and on the role that clarity and conciseness play in that purpose. However, for your words to be clear and direct, you must first have clear and undistorted thinking.

In the framework of assertive communication, it is essential to develop emotional balance points. Only in this way can desires, needs and disagreements be expressed in a clear and direct way, without affecting other people.

Many fail to reach that point of balance, due to the perspective they adopt to interpret reality. If the point of view emphasizes the negative and, depending on this, gives rise to erroneous perceptions, the predominant note is conflicting communication, rather than assertive communication. Then we'll talk about negative thoughts and the distortions of thinking that prevent assertiveness.

Negative thoughts

It is not the reality that causes emotions in a person. What is decisive is the way in which events are thought of and, consequently, the interpretation given to them. Therefore, the same situation can be perceived, felt and interpreted in very different ways by each person. The best way to illustrate this is with the famous metaphor of the glass with water in half: is it half full or is it half empty? Each person chooses.

Human beings tend to give greater importance to negative events, largely by instinct. Threatening or dangerous events call into question physical or psychological survival. That is why they have a greater impact than positive events, they remain more engraved in the memory and are more difficult to digest.

When anxiety is present, threats usually begin to be seen where there aren't any. Or the danger is exaggerated, with no basis for doing so. This psychological condition is expressed through negative thoughts. These are ideas that appear automatically to activate fear and/or anger. This, in turn, causes flight or fight responses. That's very true when the danger is real. On the other hand, if the risk is only imaginary, they lead to erratic and irrational behavior.

In this way, a person ends up thinking that a simple headache is a symptom of a brain tumor. Or that it's better not to be near the beach, because you never know when there will be a tsunami. Or perhaps, that it is better not to leave home because there are many dangers on the street. All in all, life can turn into hell.

Negative thoughts can have a lot of power. They tend to be very invasive and therefore it is not easy to control them. Often, they lead to a series of cognitive distortions that determine the way we see the world and other people.

Cognitive distortions

Cognitive distortions are mental patterns that alter the objective perception of reality. They are the favorite child of negative thoughts and can become permanent traits that condition the way you live.

These distortions grow like a weed inside you and come to significantly limit your freedom and your evolution as a human being. Cognitive distortions are a concept that we owe to the illustrious psychologist Albert Ellis, father of Rational Emotive Therapy. He defined them as "traps" of thinking that lead to an illogical and erroneous interpretation of reality.

The main cognitive distortions are as follows.

Dichotomous or polarizing thinking

This cognitive distortion is characterized by the adoption of extreme points of view, deliberately ignoring nuances. Either it's white or it's black; or it's false or it's true, etc. Like when you say: "If you're not with me, you're against me"; that is, if you don't agree with me on everything, it means that you're my enemy.

About generalization

In this case, a part of reality is taken and interpreted as if it were the whole. Something is generalized, arbitrarily. For example, someone tries to learn to dance and fails to do so in the first class; from this they infer that they are not good at dancing and that they will never be able to learn.

Labelling

Labeling is an overgeneralization brought to its maximum expression. It consists of pejoratively classifying oneself or another person and then placing or placing another person within a certain category forever. Like when a person makes some mistakes and says, "I'm stupid." Or when someone says, "All the fans on that team are ignorant."

Selective abstraction or filtering

It consists of taking an element out of its context in order to interpret it in a rigged and, generally, negative way. For example, a person is usually calm and affable. However, he is going through a difficult time and has a lot of pressure. All of a sudden, she says she's stressed. Then someone says: "I already knew that you weren't as equanimous a person as you look."

Disqualification of positive experiences

It is the tendency to place excessive emphasis on negative experiences and, at the same time, ignore positive experiences. An example: Luis scores 9/10 on an exam. They congratulate him and he says, "It was just a 9, not a 10." Or he responds with a phrase like this: "A 9 is worthless in this matter, if I have the others at 7".

Arbitrary inference

Arbitrary inference consists of taking certain assumptions for granted, when there is no evidence to support them. Within this category there are two basic modalities:

- *Divination of thought.* Supposedly, the intentions or thoughts of others are known, without this being the product of reasoning or logical inference. "If I ask for the raise, my boss will think that I am ambitious and materialistic."

- *Self-fulfilling prophecy.* It is an anticipation of negative consequences. This conditions and leads to, in effect, a negative result, due to conditioning. "If I speak in public, I'm going to stutter." The same fear causes stuttering to actually occur.

Magnification and minimization

This cognitive distortion leads to magnifying one aspect while minimizing another. It often occurs when someone with low self-esteem decides to compare themselves to another person: they see the other person's virtues greater than they are and their own as something insignificant.

Emotional Reasoning

It has to do with the inability to distinguish external reality from internal reality. Therefore, if a person feels bad, he begins to believe that everything is wrong. Or vice versa:

he assumes that everything is wrong and that is why he feels bad. For example: "I don't tolerate such injustice, but I can't do anything because I have no power."

The categorical imperatives

Categorical imperatives are inflexible beliefs about what you or others should be like. They favor relentless self-criticism, if they are directed at the person themselves, or resentment and anger, if they are directed at others. They are expressed in expressions such as "Should" or "I should". The person says to himself "I should stop smoking" and because he doesn't, he feels guilty or frustrated. It is recommended to replace the "Should" with "I Would Like" or the "I Would Like".

Personalization or false attribution

It occurs when a person assumes that it is the cause of negative events that are not actually under their control. Also when you feel alluded to if someone makes a negative comment, even if it doesn't really have anything to do with it. For example: "Stay away from me. I give people bad luck." Or "They say it in the ear because they are speaking ill of me."

Catastrophic Vision

It happens when someone anticipates the outcome of events, assuming that it will be disastrous. Or when he assumes that something very bad will happen to him, without knowing why. For example: "There are a lot of companies that are going bankrupt. The same thing can happen at any time in the company where I work. They'll throw me out into the street..."

Control fallacy

It takes place in two ways. The first is when you assume that you are in control, above all, without it being the case. Example: "I haven't been able to get my child to change. I'm a disaster as a mother." Or it also appears on the contrary, when it is assumed that there is nothing to do, when in reality it is possible to intervene in something. For example, "Climate change will wipe out human beings. It doesn't matter what I do."

The fallacy of change

It consists of assuming that if there is a difficulty, nothing can be done until the situation or person with whom you have that problem changes. "Until you're punctual, I'm not going to feel comfortable." Or "As long as I don't have a fair boss, my efforts to move up the job are worthless."

Divine reward fallacy

This fallacy occurs when some hidden force is expected to provide or improve something in the future, even if one remains passive. "Someday life will reward me for the hard times I've been through." "Sooner or later that person will pay for stealing from me."

In short...

The persistence of negative thoughts leads to the formation of erroneous mental patterns. These are known as cognitive distortions and are erroneous ways of perceiving and processing reality. This is largely due to the tendency to lock ourselves in a personal bubble, regardless of what is happening outside of ourselves.

One of the ways to counter this trend is active listening. This ability helps you connect with others in a deeper and more genuine way. In doing so, you begin to realize that many of your thought patterns don't match up with reality. How to develop active listening? We'll see you soon.

2.5 How to develop active listening skills

"Wisdom comes when you are able to calm down. Just watch, just listen. There is no need for anything else. Stilling, watching and listening activates the non-conceptual intelligence that lies within you. Let stillness guide your words and actions." -Eckhart Tolle-

Active listening is defined as a mode of listening whose purpose is to understand the other. To achieve this, the focus is on the other person, rather than on what is going to be said or answered. This leads to your interlocutor feeling listened to and, therefore, comforted when talking to you.

This type of listening improves communication and promotes understanding. It also helps to develop bonds of trust and reduces the risk of conflict. FBI detectives have pointed out that active listening techniques have been very useful to them during kidnapping negotiations.

In addition, teachers, psychologists and even marketers benefit a lot from active listening. Much of the tensions that occur in everyday relationships could be managed and alleviated through this type of listening.

How to develop active listening? The following are some of the tools you can use to acquire or improve your active listening skills.

Don't interrupt the other person while they're talking

The golden rule of active listening is precisely that of listening. Therefore, it is very important that you put aside any thoughts that appear while the other person is talking. You should refrain from interrupting the other person, unless there is a good reason. For example, that you didn't understand something.

Avoid judgments and advice

At the heart of active listening is the acceptance of the other. If you start to make positive or negative judgments, it means that you are more attentive to your internal dialogue than to the other person's words. You must neither make judgments nor give answers. The latter includes advice.

Paraphrase and summarize

You just have to repeat in your own words the most important aspects of what the other person said, summarizing the message. This helps you check if you really understood what they wanted to tell you. On the other hand, it is evidence that you have actually listened. It's an excellent tool for connecting deeply with the other person.

Redirect the conversation, if necessary

If your interlocutor starts to ramble or loses track of their central idea, the active listener is there to help you focus again. It's also evidence that you're listening carefully and that your goal is to make it easier for the other person to express themselves fully.

Adopt positive nonverbal language

Non-verbal language must communicate two ideas in particular. One, that you're open to what the other person has to say. Therefore, you should avoid locking or closing body positions, such as crossing your arms. The second idea you communicate with active listening is that you approve of the other. A frown or facial gesture of rejection breaks the connection.

Question

The question plays two central roles in active listening. On the one hand, it shows that you are connected to the other person. On the other hand, encourage your interlocutor to continue talking or to delve deeper into some aspect. Use closed questions to corroborate the information or point out a matter. Open-ended questions, on the other hand, are the right ones to expand or complement the central topic.

Find the deep meaning

A person speaks to you not only with ideas, but also with the heart. Much of what he has to say is not expressed through words, but also through attitudes, gestures, tone of voice, etc. An active listener is attentive to all these signals and, in this way, manages to capture the profound meaning of what the other person is saying.

Respond to feelings and not to words

Based on the above, in active listening you should be more attentive to the emotions involved than to the words. You respond to those emotions and not to words. If the other person says to you "I don't know what to do", the right thing is not to respond with instructions, but with an empathetic gesture: "It must be a big burden for you not to know which path to take".

It helps to clarify

To listen actively is to be involved in the expression of the other. That is why it is valid to help that person to clarify what they think and feel. The best way to do this is with questions or suggestions for reflection: "If you don't know what to do, maybe you could first think about what not to do."

Use positive reinforcements

Although it may seem trivial, a person who is sincerely stating what they feel and think needs gestures of approval to move forward. Words such as "I understand" or gestures such as nodding are very useful to make the other person feel comfortable and confident.

Respect the silences

People turn to silence as a means to think a little better. Also, to evaluate if they say or stop saying something. They are part of free expression. Because of this, it is best to respect those moments when the other person stops talking. It is important to avoid the temptation to fill those silences with any word, as if there were haste or fear of a break in communication.

Avoid these mistakes

There are three typical mistakes that someone not very experienced can make.

- The first is to be condescending to the other person or to "bring him the idea".

- The second is to try to minimize the importance of what they tell you, with the aim of comforting the other, as when you say "don't worry about that".

- Third, to become anxious if the other person cries or has a very obvious emotional manifestation.

They are all mistakes because they indicate that you are not focused on the other, but on your own emotions and beliefs.

Use active listening when appropriate

Active listening should not be practiced all the time, as it would be exhausting and often unnecessary. This skill is particularly relevant for resolving conflicts, finding solutions to a problem situation, moderating meetings, increasing collaboration or developing negotiation.

Practical exercises to improve effective communication

The time has come to exercise the skills we have discussed in this chapter. As always, our recommendation is that you be disciplined and persevering to obtain visible results. Hands to work.

Speech clarity exercises

This group of exercises aims to improve the way you speak, from a physical point of view. Practice them daily, especially if you think you have problems in this regard.

Blow paper balls

Make three medium-sized paper balls and place them on a surface. Then, take a straw or straw and blow it to make them move from one point to another. Repeat for three minutes. This is a way to stimulate the muscles in your mouth and will help you improve your diction.

Pronounce vocals

Breathe in air through your nose with your mouth closed and then breathe out slowly. While doing the latter, pronounce all five vowels, taking care to vocalize them very well, so that they are clearly understood. It will help you with vocalization.

The language

This is another exercise you should do daily if you have difficulty vocalizing or projecting your voice well. You only have to make 10 turns with your tongue, in all directions. Then, stretch your tongue out and then bring it to the palate. Repeat 10 times.

Modulation and speed

To better modulate and speak at an appropriate speed, it is best to practice with tongue twisters. Also, it's a good idea to pick up a book and read a paragraph, more or less long. First, read it very slowly. Then, increase the speed a little and then read as fast as you can. Compare.

Lips and facial muscles

Inflate your cheeks and pass the air from one side to the other for one minute. Then, take a pencil and place it between your teeth. Start speaking or read a text, trying to make sure all the words you're saying are understood. Repeat this exercise three times.

Language fluency exercises

Language fluency exercises are intended to improve your language management, so that you can be more and more clear and concise. Practice them as often as possible.

Synonyms and antonyms

Ask a person to say a word to you and think of all the synonyms you can remember first. Then, point out the antonyms. Finally, consult a dictionary of synonyms and antonyms to complement your work. There are many that you can find online.

Awareness of expression

This is an exercise that will probably bring you many surprises. Think of a topic that you know well and come up with a short three-minute dissertation. Record yourself talking. Then, think about what problems you may be having with your oral expression. The best thing is to repeat the exercise by recording yourself on video. So you can appreciate your non-verbal language as well.

Synthesis

Listen carefully to any voice message they sent you. If you don't have that possibility, then choose to listen to a live radio program. Then, state the central idea of what you heard, in a single sentence. Also, choose a long sentence that you've heard and rephrase it with fewer words.

Schemes and mind maps

Watch a short video or a news story on television. Then try to represent the content of what you saw on a mind map. Indicate what the central idea was, the secondary ideas and the tertiary ideas. Graph it as if it were an organization chart.

Exposing an idea

Prepare a short five-minute presentation on a topic you know and like. Make an outline or mind map. Do your dissertation and record yourself. Then, evaluate your strengths and weaknesses when you speak.

Negative thinking exercises and cognitive distortions

These exercises will help you become aware of inappropriate thinking patterns. Carry them out whenever you can.

Identifying Negative Thoughts

At night, try to remember if you had any negative thoughts during the day. Write it down. Do the same for a week and then evaluate. Are there thoughts that are repeated? What are the phrases you use to express such thoughts? Raising awareness will help you eradicate those ideas.

Cognitive distortions

Give an example of each of the negative distortions we address in this chapter. If the example has to do with yourself, all the better.

Active listening exercises

Active listening exercises serve to train the basic skills of this assertive communication tool. Try to practice them, especially in the context of disagreements or conflict situations.

Paraphrase and questions

During a conversation, paraphrase what your interlocutor is saying. You should not repeat his words exactly, but rather say the ideas on your own terms. Also, ask at least one open question and one closed question. Try to capture the other person's reaction when you do all of this.

Listening without judging

After a spontaneous conversation with someone you know very little or with whom you don't have the best relationship, write down the judgments you made mentally about that person. Reflect on this question: what do these judgments bring to communication with that interlocutor?

Conclusion

In this chapter we have discussed the importance of filling our words with content, avoiding falling into empty speeches that, in most cases, only talk about lack of concentration and anxiety. We also referred to the importance of clarity and conciseness. Finally, we deal with the topics of cognitive distortions and active listening.

You should not forget the following points:

- Empty speeches are characterized by being repetitive, scattered, rhetorical and dense. They are avoided by thinking before speaking, listening, being more specific and raising the linguistic level.

- Clarity and conciseness are the virtues par excellence in effective communication.

- The best way to be more clear and concise is to plan what you are going to say, think about your interlocutor, keep in mind the context and adequately control verbal and non-verbal language.

- Negative thoughts are irrational beliefs that stem from unresolved fears or anger. They give rise to cognitive distortions. The latter make it impossible to make an objective assessment of reality.

- Active listening is essential in the framework of assertive communication. There are several techniques that allow it to be developed. These include paraphrasing, questioning and affective decoding.

In the next chapter we are going to look at one of the most interesting and useful topics in assertive communication: persuasive speech. We will discuss the best methods for you to become a great speaker and to successfully speak in public. Don't miss it!

CHAPTER 3: BECOMING A PERSUASIVE TALKER

"The art of persuading consists both in the art of pleasing and of convincing; since men are governed more by whim than by reason." -Blaise Pascal-

Demosthenes is considered the greatest orator of all time. This great Greek politician began his career in the midst of great adversity. His first speech was a resounding failure. Not only was he unable to thread his ideas coherently, but he was also mocked by the public for one of his faults: he was a stutterer.

Fate felt sorry for this orphan and poor young man. A teacher arrived in his life who instilled in him a decisive idea: it was not natural gifts, but hard work that would lead him to achieve his dream of being a great orator and politician.

Demosthenes is said to have begun a tenacious struggle. He eliminated his social life and began practicing his speeches from dawn. In the afternoon, he would run along the beaches screaming at the sun, to learn to project his voice. At night, she would fill her mouth with pebbles and put a knife between her teeth to overcome stuttering. After a while, he achieved his mission. He became the most brilliant speaker of his time. Cicero himself defined him as "the perfect speaker".

In this chapter we are going to talk about the wonderful ability to persuade with speech. First we are going to refer to public speaking. Then we'll talk about one of the hot topics in today's world: public speaking. We'll tell you how you can gain confidence to do so and what are the most appropriate techniques. Next, we will refer to persuasion and negotiation techniques. As always, we will finish the chapter by offering you some exercises that will help you develop your skills.

3.1 Traits of a good speaker and one-on-one persuasion

"A speaker is one who says what he thinks and feels what he says."
-William J. Bryan-

Quintilian was considered the best oratory teacher in the world in Ancient Rome. He instructed several emperors, including the famous Hadrian. He wrote a classic work called Oratory Institutions and there he pointed out that "clarity is the first virtue of eloquence".

Cicero, another of the great Roman teachers of oratory, in his treatise On the Speaker, pointed out that the three great virtues of the speaker were: correctness (puritas), elegance (ornatus) and adequacy (aptum). Both Quintilian and Cicero offered key points that are still valid.

Oratory can be defined as the art of persuading, moving and delighting. Thus, its objective is to convince and produce changes in emotions. The latter are the real engine of action. This is achieved through enjoyment with words.

Types of oratory

Like all art, public speaking needs practice. Becoming a great speaker involves mastering knowledge and skills associated with language, psychology, emotional intelligence and kinesiology, among others. However, there are several types of oratory and each of them requires different skills.

The main types of oratory are the following:

- Politics. It is the most traditional. Used by figures of power to convince others of their ideology and their projects.

- Religious. The one used in religious services to spread the faith.

- Business. It is also known as "Management Speaking" and is focused on achieving corporate objectives.

- Legal. It includes the oratory used in trials to present the arguments of the parties involved.

- Social. It corresponds to everyday situations and is used to express emotions.

- Pedagogical. The one used by teachers in order to transmit knowledge and knowledge.

- Artistic. It is the one used in show business and the media. Its purpose is to cheer up and generate some kind of aesthetic pleasure.

- Military. It refers to the oratory used in armed forces to inculcate the values proper to service or motivate for action.

The good speaker

The speaker is any person who speaks before an audience. Its purpose is to cause some kind of effect on the audience to whom your message is addressed. It seeks to convince them of an idea or belief, communicate a discovery or finding, motivating, arousing interest in something, alert, posing a problem, etc. What are the characteristics of a good speaker? Let's see.

Physical characteristics

A good speaker has physical or bodily abilities that help him to convey his message in a more coherent or powerful way. It includes the following:

- Personal presentation. The speaker's clothing must be appropriate to the event and the audience.

- Good voice projection. It is necessary to speak in a tone that corresponds to the type of message being given. In general terms, the high tone excites and energizes, while the low tone calls for reflection.

- Diction. It is very important for the speaker to pronounce the words correctly, so that they are understood perfectly. Otherwise, your message will be lost.

- Speech speed or rhythm. Speak quickly when you want to vitalize the public. Slow, if the goal is to incite reflection. A good rhythm is one that combines both styles, in a harmonious and coherent way.

- Body language. The speaker must exhibit a position of control over space and authority in front of the public. The best thing to do is to move little and with intention.

- Gestures. Facial gestures serve to accompany the message given with words. It also energizes the exhibition.

- Eye contact. It is best for the speaker to maintain visual contact with the entire audience, focusing on different segments of the audience throughout his speech.

Intellectual characteristics

The basic intellectual characteristics are two. The first is excellent knowledge and preparation of the subject to be discussed. Ideas must be argued with solid arguments or evidence. At the same time, the development of the topic must be orderly and coherent. The best thing is that the exhibition also has a good color. This is achieved through the use of examples, striking facts and anecdotes.

The second important intellectual characteristic is a good command of the language. The experienced speaker has a wide vocabulary and constructs sentences correctly. It is fluid and has the capacity to explain the subject in a clear, concise and understandable way for all types of audience.

Psychological characteristics

A good speaker must project self-confidence, at all times. You must also be empathetic to capture the public's interests and the possible reactions your speech may generate. Your attitude needs to be positive and open, so that you can connect with your audience.

Being imaginative and sensitive can help you a lot in carrying out an intervention that captures the interest, motivates and moves the emotions of those who see and hear you. Finally, it's very important to be honest: if you don't know something, you'll say so. Its purpose is to convey ideas and emotions, not to manipulate people.

3.2 Persuasion and one-on-one negotiation techniques

"You will win, but you will not convince. You will win because you have plenty of brute force; but you will not convince, because convincing means persuading. And to persuade, you need something that you lack: reason and right in the fight." -Miguel de Unamuno-

Persuasion and negotiation are natural components of any communication process. Every time you present an idea or try to reach an agreement, you are making use of these tools. However, you do it spontaneously and that's why you don't notice it.

The truth is that both the word persuasion and the term negotiation are unfriendly to many people. The act of persuading is often confused with the act of manipulating. In the same way, it is sometimes believed that negotiating is trying to get the most out of yourself. Neither one nor the other corresponds to reality.

What differentiates persuasion from manipulation is a decisive factor: intentionality. Persuading is convincing someone to believe or do something. It is transparent and uses argument and seduction to achieve the objective. In manipulation, on the other hand, there is a hidden objective. A person is induced to believe or do something, but using deception.

Intentions also come into play in negotiation. From the point of view of assertive communication, good negotiation takes place when both sides win something. The objective is to find a balance between one's own needs and desires, versus those of the other. If we only want to satisfy our own interests, we are not talking about negotiation, but rather about fraud or ruse. Soon we will talk about all this in greater detail.

The Principles of Persuasion

The renowned American psychologist Robert Cialdini is one of the most renowned experts on the subject of persuasion and negotiation. In his work Influence, the Psychology of Persuasion established the six principles of persuasion. They are the following.

- **Social approval**. He points out that the people around us and those we admire have the greatest influence on us.

- **Authority**. Experienced or more famous people or sources exert more influence on others. Shakira's opinions, even if they are the same as those of the neighbor, carry more weight.

- **Scarcity**. If people perceive that something is scarce, they will be more likely to acquire it. If a company releases a "limited edition" of a product, it is very likely that more people will want to buy it.

- **Sympathy**. People are more influenced by those they like. All the commercials show "nice" people.

- **Commitment and coherence**. People want to be consistent with others. It is possible to persuade someone by appealing to their desire for consistency. "Didn't you say you wanted to buy a quality car? So why are you reluctant to pay a little more?"

- **Reciprocity**. If one person receives a benefit from another, they will feel a desire to reciprocate. This is the basic principle of "free samples".

Persuasion techniques

To be persuasive, you don't have to have great charisma, or become famous. Assertive communication, in general, is an excellent strategy for producing convincing and profitable interactions. However, there are also some specific techniques that you can use in different situations. Get to know them and practice them. Some of them are the following.

Choose the right context

The context is favorable if it allows them to express themselves freely and without pressure. When either of you is in a hurry, or you are on the street in the middle of a storm, it will not be easy to persuade your interlocutor of anything. This should be taken into account by salespeople who call you in the middle of the morning, when you have a thousand things to think about. We have to be timely.

Make your interlocutor feel comfortable

Take the first few minutes to make your interlocutor feel comfortable. The goal is to reduce tension and make both of you feel relaxed. Give her a compliment or let her notice how beautiful the afternoon is. Make a casual and friendly comment about the environment. Comment on some anecdote associated with similar situations.

Establish an alliance

Both to begin to persuade and to start a negotiation, the first thing is to establish an alliance with your interlocutor. That is, a common goal. The other person wants to buy a car and you sell them: there is a common point there. Or she likes movies and so do you, why not go together? The examples are endless.

Encourages empathy

Do you remember the principle of sympathy? People are more influenced by those they "like". You should know that people are more sympathetic to those people who find similar to themselves. In a subtle way, you can begin to imitate the other. Paraphrase what they say and copy some of their body language. You'll see how you start to sympathize with him.

Express yourself positively

It is quite natural for a disagreement to appear during a conversation. However, you should be careful to offer a frontal opposition. If you want to persuade someone, avoid direct confrontation.

In the face of a disagreement, you have two paths. The first is to redirect the subject to something they think about in a similar way. The second is to use phrases such as "Although I don't agree with you on everything, I think you're right in this regard" and move on to another point.

Use an inclusive and collaborative approach

It is very important that your interlocutor feels included in your reasoning and that they perceive you as an ally. This can be achieved by focusing on aspects such as calling him by name and showing interest using active listening tools (such as paraphrasing and questions). If the other person sees you as someone who is on their side, they'll be more open to your suggestions.

Use weakness as an advantage

Strangely enough, the best thing to do is to openly show your weaknesses. On the one hand, that gives you added reliability and credibility. On the other hand, it eliminates the possibility for your interlocutor to attack, criticize or oppose you based on such weaknesses. The best thing is to learn to show those weaknesses as if they were advantages.

For example, if you want to sell your house, but it has a noticeable defect in the bathroom, don't wait for your potential buyer to discover it. Mention it directly and tell him that it would be a great opportunity to remodel that area. He adds that this is the reason you had to lower the selling price, otherwise the house would be worth more.

Use emotional language

In the field of persuasion, emotions are much more important than ideas. Therefore, you should focus on what your interlocutor is feeling, regardless of what their words say.

Based on what you observe, present arguments that appeal to that emotional state that you detect in the other.

A formula that does not fail is to appeal to three values that have proven to have an important impact on people: justice, freedom and responsibility. Phrases like "This is the most responsible offer I can make you", or "Feel free to tell me what you don't like", etc., tend to have a lot of power.

Use speed to your advantage

In persuasive communication, there is one premise that never fails: good news comes slowly and bad news comes quickly. So, if you're going to talk about something that's very positive for the other person, go into detail and savor every word. On the other hand, if you have to refer to something negative, use a few words and change the subject quickly. Your message will be more persuasive.

Two Negotiation Tips

All persuasion techniques are useful to advance negotiations in any field. However, when negotiating with someone, you must also take into account two realities that you should not lose sight of.

First of all, you must be aware that negotiating involves being willing to compromise. If you are not, it means that you do not want a negotiation, but rather impose yourself. At the same time, you need to be clear about the aspects that you do not consider negotiable. The more aware you are both of the points where you can give in and what you are not willing to do so on, the better the outcome of this process will be.

Secondly, there are many negotiations that do not produce the expected fruit immediately. This process can take several days, weeks, or even months. Therefore, whenever there is a meeting with the person you are negotiating with, you should conclude by leaving the doors open when you come in.

The last impression should be pleasant. Ideally, if possible, you should introduce a positive expectation for the future: "I loved talking to you and I'm going to think of an offer that you can't resist." It usually works very well.

3.5 Practical exercises to improve the ability to speak in public

Practicing is the best way to gain public speaking skills. There is no other way to develop your full potential. The fruits of perseverance are always much juicier than those of chance. Next, we propose some exercises to increase your skills in this area.

Self-confidence exercises

As we noted before, the more you speak in public, the more confidence you gain in yourself to do so. The following exercises can help you with that task.

Practicing relaxation

Relaxation exercises are very useful for reducing nervousness, under all circumstances. Breathing is key to this purpose. A good technique to reduce fear before a public presentation is the following.

Take a plastic bag and insert your mouth and nose into the opening. Close it so that no air escapes. Start breathing deeply. The bag should inflate and compress, with the rhythm of your breathing. Repeat three times and rest for one minute. Then perform the entire cycle four more times. You'll feel more relaxed when you're done.

The three individual essays

The more you rehears a presentation, the more confident you'll feel about your performance. There are three types of tests that you can do on your own and that will be very useful:

Talk to the wall. Just start saying what you remember about your exhibition in front of a wall, without focusing too much on whether it's exactly the same as you planned it. The feeling you experience in front of that wall is similar to what you'll feel in front of your audience.

Talk to the mirror. Repeat the previous exercise, but this time do it in front of the mirror. Evaluate your sign and body language.

Film yourself. Do the same exercise, but this time try to stick to the script of your exhibition and correct the errors detected in front of the mirror. Then, watch the recording carefully and take note only of the strengths you see in yourself.

Doing all three types of rehearsals is very useful, especially for those who are very afraid to face the public. Don't omit any.

Small audiences

When you have your presentation well prepared and you feel ready to face an audience, do your intervention, as planned, in front of a small group of friends or relatives. At the end, ask them for written feedback. Assume with objectivity and maturity what they point out to you.

Persuasion exercises

These exercises aim to familiarize you with persuasion techniques, so that you can apply them more and more naturally.

The Principles of Persuasion

Look for an example that illustrates each of the principles of persuasion proposed by Robert Cialdini. Think about the reasons why they work.

Persuasion techniques

Do the following activities:

In a casual conversation, try subtly imitating the language and gestures of your interlocutor. Make a mental note of their reactions. Then, do just the opposite: use language and gestures that are very different from those of the person you're talking to. Observe their reaction.

Identify the type of alliance you can make with each of the people you live with and with your closest co-workers. That is: find a positive common goal.

At least once a day, pay attention to the emotions of someone you're talking to. Try to focus on what that person is feeling and not on what they are saying. If you do it often, you'll become more and more proficient in emotional language.

Apply the persuasion techniques that are most striking to you in a disagreement or negotiation that you are carrying out. Whether you achieve your goal or not, evaluate what happened as objectively as possible.

3.3 How to develop the confidence to speak in front of several people

"According to most studies, people's number one fear is public speaking. Number two is death. Death is number two. Does it sound good? This means for the average person, if you're going to a funeral, you're better off in the casket than doing the eulogy." -Jerry Seinfield-

As the chapter points out, some people are more afraid of speaking in public than of dying. This is not an exaggeration. There are not a few people who suffer a panic attack if they have to go to an audience. There are also many who systematically refrain from expressing themselves, out of fear of facing the monster with a thousand heads.

Fear causes your voice, hands and legs to tremble. When you realize that you're trembling and that it shows, you get more scared. Then your mouth dries out, you stop controlling your breathing, and it's even possible that a tick or a ridiculous movement will appear. The audience bursts into laughter and that's when you have to run away, take your passport and take the first plane that leaves for a country that nobody knows... Don't take it seriously: we're exaggerating, but that's what fear is: exaggerated.

The good news is that you don't have to go through all of that: fear can be controlled. You need practice: the more you overcome your fear of speaking in front of others, the easier it will be for you to overcome it. And vice versa. How to do it? Next, we'll talk about some of the most effective techniques to increase self-confidence when speaking in public.

Prepare the topic: The Golden Key

The ultimate way to increase your self-confidence is to prepare yourself well before speaking in public. There is no substitute for this. Yes or yes, you have to make a lot of effort to be ready, at the right time. You have to take the bull by the horns.

First, get very informed and collect quality information about the topic you are going to talk about. Consult several sources and make sure you fully understand what each one is proposing. Get interesting or little-known facts about the subject. Then, select the information you are going to use; filter out everything that is unnecessary.

Never, listen carefully: NEVER try to speak in public about a topic you don't know. It is the direct path to disaster. The more afraid you are, the better you should prepare your topic.

Make a script

Once you have all the information and you've decided on it, sit down for a moment and think. It defines three aspects: what is the central idea? What are you looking for when making your presentation? What would be the logical order of it?

Once you've answered those questions, come up with a written script. It's a kind of script, as if you were an actor and those are the lines you have to say to play your role. It is very important that you believe in what you are going to say. If you don't, no one will believe you either. Read your script several times, aloud.

Take care of yourself and relax

A week before your public intervention, place special emphasis on your self-care. Eat well, sleep well, and get some physical activity. Take five minutes a day to breathe deeply in a place where no one will disturb you. If possible, take a "forest bath", that is, a walk through a large garden or green area. Think about everything positive you have and are. Keep away any hint of unnecessary negative thoughts or self-criticism.

Get to know the environment beforehand

Go to the place where you will do your intervention and examine it carefully. Familiarize yourself with that space. If possible, test microphones and equipment. If for some reason this is not possible, arrive early on the day of the exhibition anyway to observe the site and test the devices. It's always good to have a plan B in mind, in case the sound, the video beam or any of the technological resources you're going to use don't work.

Learn to hide your nerves

There are many cases in which the speaker is dying of fear, but the audience doesn't notice it. Sometimes that trembling in the hands is not so obvious, even if it seems so to you. However, avoid taking anything in your hands, just in case. If you feel your voice trembling, take a short pause and breathe. If you do, the shaking will stop. If people's faces intimidate you, look to the back of the auditorium, to a specific point where you don't see anyone. That's it.

Use your body

Several studies have indicated that body posture is closely associated with the emotions that are experienced. Therefore, if you feel insecure, this will reflect on your posture. But at the same time, if you adopt a safe stance, this will modify your emotions. It is recommended that you adopt a "power pose". That is, upright, with the chest out and the arms loose on both sides of the body. You can also make a jug with your arms. Adopting that pose will make you feel more confident.

Concentrate

Concentration is essential so that your nerves don't play tricks on you. If you focus decisively on the subject you are talking about, the fear will most likely dissipate. On the other hand, if you start to notice the expression of people in the front row, or the income of those who arrived late or anything else, the risk of increased nervousness increases.

Slow down the speed

Try to speak slowly. Not only is it something your audience will be very grateful for, but it also helps you to be less nervous. In the same way, it is best to move slowly and slowly. Seeing someone walking from one side of the stage to the other or making quick movements with their hands or head causes some tension.

Move forward step by step

Great speakers make jokes, tell anecdotes with great grace and are able to manage an impeccable rhythm during their presentations. It's very likely that you'll get to that, but you need time. If you feel insecure, don't try to "play funny" to make your intervention more attractive. Better go little by little. Give color to what you say and tell a story or two, but don't intend to make a show if you don't have enough experience yet. Time to time.

3.4 Techniques for speaking and communicating effectively in front of several people

"If you don't feel comfortable speaking in public, and no one starts out comfortable; you have to learn to be comfortable, practice. I can't overstate the importance of practicing." -Hillary Clinton-

The determining factor for communicating effectively with a group or audience is the confidence you have in yourself, together with the fact that you know your subject well. That said, it's also important to know useful techniques to make your intervention as complete, clear and pleasant as possible.

Hundreds of books have been written on the subject, but we know that you are looking for practical knowledge. That's why we'll soon let you know the strategies you can use to succeed when speaking in front of other people.

Basic preparation

We have already mentioned the importance of preparing yourself well before speaking in front of several people. To that said, we should add some important elements that you should consider during the planning process. They are the following.

- **What**. Have clear and memorized the central idea of the intervention, as well as the three most relevant secondary ideas.

- **To whom**. You need to know how many people are going to listen to you and what their main characteristics are. This will help you to nuance your speech.

- **Time planning.** You must define the length of time your intervention will last. Ideally, you should also set aside a certain amount of time for each of the components that make it up (introduction, development, conclusion).

- **Examples and anecdotes.** Include some examples and/or anecdotes to oxygenate the presentation of your content. They go a long way in capturing or regaining the public's attention. They also give your intervention a more dynamic and appropriate rhythm.

- **Resources.** It refers to technological or other tools, which you are going to use to make your intervention. These aids must serve a specific purpose. They are not used just for the sake of it.

Startup techniques

When you have prepared the topic and defined the basic elements, the next thing is to specify what the beginning of your intervention will be like. This aspect is decisive, since the way you start will generate an impression that will be reflected in the rest of your intervention. Therefore, you must carefully choose the technique to be employed.

There are several ways to start an exhibition. It is recommended that you choose the one that best suits the topic or best corresponds to your objective. In general terms, you can choose one of the following options:

- **Phraseological.** It consists of starting by bringing up a phrase or a quote from a famous author. It is very suitable when you are going to expose something new or controversial, which requires support from some authority on the subject.

- **Anecdotal.** You should only tell a story, real or fictional, associated with the subject. It is usually used to arouse emotions, in addition to capturing interest and motivating. It is very suitable if you will be dealing with a humanistic topic.

- **Humorous.** Here you can use a phrase, a story or something that is hilarious to the public. It helps to relax the environment and reduce nerves. It's a suitable start for almost any type of topic.

- **Interrogative**. It consists of starting by asking a question that will induce reflection in those present. It is very well suited to new topics or in cases where your goal is to persuade the public of an idea or belief.

- **Dramatized**. The public imagination is usually used. The speaker makes a basic representation of some everyday situation. It usually immediately captures people's attention. It is widely used in the marketing field.

Development techniques

For the development of the topic, you can choose three basic strategies: inductive, deductive or analog. As in other cases, the choice depends on the subject you are going to work on, the audience you are targeting and the objectives you are pursuing. Also, of course, you should always consider which one makes you feel more comfortable.

Inductive technique

It consists of dealing with the subject moving from the particular to the general. This means that you start from a specific premise or case and develop the topic in such a way that this allows you to arrive at a general statement. It is usually appropriate for technical or scientific topics.

For example, if you talk about pollution, you could start by quoting the everyday habits of an average family. Based on this, you address the consequences that this generates and how, together with other factors, they end up causing a large-scale polluting effect.

Deductive technique

The deductive technique is the opposite of the previous one. In this case, you develop the topic based on a premise or a general case, and then arrive at a specific statement or situation. It is almost always used to deal with social or humanistic issues.

For example, you are going to talk about citizen insecurity. To do this, you start by giving data on this phenomenon in the world, or pointing out how it has evolved over time. Then, you can focus on insecurity in contemporary cities, until you get to the way it affects each individual. In other words, you first show the panorama and then the photo in the foreground.

Analog technique

The analogical technique consists of exposing the subject by establishing contrasts or comparisons between two or more realities. It's usually very useful when your goal is to prove a certain argument or persuade something specific.

For example, you are going to talk about the healthcare system in Japan. To do so, you can compare each of the aspects that make up such a system, with the same elements in another country's health system. This resource helps highlight the aspects you want to highlight.

Conclusion techniques

The conclusion of your speech is as important as the introduction and development of the topic. It is a way of rounding off what has been said and of leaving a certain impression on the audience. Some of the techniques to make a proper and impactful closure are the following:

- **Phraseological**. You end the presentation with a phrase or quote from some authority on the subject you discussed. Your goal is to reiterate the central idea, support it or encourage reflection.

- **Emotional**. It consists of concluding by appealing to some basic emotion: fear, love, anger, enthusiasm, etc. Like when someone ends up saying "Long live recycling!", or "We will not tolerate any more injustices!", etc.

- **Interrogative**. In this case, you end up asking your audience a question. The question is usually asked to reaffirm an idea, invite reflection or leave a controversy raised.

- **Out of gratitude**. It is one of the most conventional forms of conclusion. The speaker thanked the public for their attention and expressed the hope that the presentation was useful. It is usually used within the framework of a social event.

- **Mixed**. It is a type of conclusion in which two or more of the above techniques are combined. For example, a phrase followed by an expression of gratitude. Or a question, followed by an emotional conclusion.

Conclusion

Assertive communication applies both to conversations between two people and to presentations in front of a group or to a wider audience. By applying the right principles and techniques, you can increase your ability to empower yourself and persuade others.

Based on what is seen in this chapter, keep the following points in mind:

- A good speaker is not born, but is made. To become one, it is necessary to comply with a series of physical, intellectual and psychological characteristics.

- Most people are afraid to speak in public. The best way to gain confidence to do so is to prepare yourself well, exercise self-care, manage nervousness, and practice frequently.

- Techniques for speaking in front of other people include preparing for the introduction, developing and concluding the topic.

- To persuade is to convince and not to manipulate. Negotiating is finding the best formula for the parties involved to win something.

- The principles of persuasion, according to Robert Cialdini, are: social approval, authority, scarcity, sympathy, commitment and coherence, and reciprocity.

- Persuasion is achieved by applying techniques such as establishing alliances, positive expression, using emotional language and empathy, among others.

- Every negotiation involves giving in to something and sometimes involves a long-term process.

In the next chapter we will talk about a topic that interests all of us: assertive leadership. We will see how it is exercised and how it is applied in specific situations, such as conflict resolution and motivation. We recommend you read it. It will be fantastic!

CHAPTER 4: BEING A STRESS-FREE LEADER

"Great leaders get out of the way to increase the self-esteem of their people. If people believe in themselves, it's incredible what they can achieve."
-Sam Walton, American businessman and founder of the Walmart chain of stores-

Nelson Mandela was one of the great leaders of our time. He achieved what was an impossible objective for many: taking the definitive step to resolve a racial conflict that had been present for more than a century in his country. He succeeded in getting enemies to sit down at the table and find common ground. He managed to change the history of South Africa, based on patience, understanding and empathy.

His life was a real feat. He spent almost 30 years in prison and many of them were completely incommunicado. During the first year of his imprisonment, his mother and eldest son died, but the authorities did not allow him to attend funerals. He got out of jail with a laudable purpose: peace. He succeeded after hard work. Everyone agrees that Mandela was not just an ideologue or a strategist, but primarily an inspirational leader.

In this chapter we will talk about assertive leadership, the same one practiced by Mandela and which made him the first black ruler of his country. We'll see what skills it requires and how intelligent authority is exercised. We'll also talk about the best techniques for delegating, motivating and resolving conflicts.

4.1 Developing assertive leadership skills

"The leader's task is to get people from where they are to where they haven't been." -Henry Kissinger-

Assertive leadership is a management style in which emotional intelligence is used to project authority in a constructive way, through efficient communication that takes into account the needs and interests of the people led. It is one of the most effective forms of leadership, since it helps to bring out the best in the team.

In assertive leadership, the objective is to establish a balance between two decisive aspects. The first is a sense of commitment to decisions; this includes compliance with tasks and compliance with limits and rules. The second is open and healthy communication, which includes aspects such as free expression, empathy and respect.

Capabilities and abilities of the assertive leader

The first virtue of an assertive leader is self-confidence. This, of course, implies that there is a strong self-esteem. Without these two elements, there can be neither assertiveness nor leadership. If the person who leads a team has no faith in their own performance, it will be difficult to get others to believe in the guidelines and orders they give.

Self-confidence is the very essence of assertiveness, but in addition to this, other skills are required to exercise leadership. The most important are the following.

Assertive communication

Let us remember that assertive communication is a style of communication in which there is a clear, frank and direct expression of thoughts and emotions, without feeling guilty and taking into account the needs and desires of others.

The assertive leader must have great communication skills. You don't need to be an expert speaker, but you should know how to express yourself clearly and concisely. Many problems in the performance of a team arise because there is no clarity about what is expected of each individual, nor about what should or should not be done in the work environment. Clarity, above other virtues, is fundamental.

Empathy

There is no assertiveness without empathy. This is the ability to put yourself in the other person's shoes and understand their cognitive and emotional perspective. An assertive leader has this skill very developed and is therefore able to understand each member of the team. This allows you to motivate them more effectively and get the best out of them.

According to Daniel Goleman (2003), empathy is fundamental in today's world of work, for three reasons. The first is that teamwork is increasingly relevant. The second is that the world is gradually becoming more globalized and this requires being open to understanding by people from all kinds of cultures. The third is that it is increasingly important to retain talent in organizations. High staff turnover is never convenient.

Other abilities and virtues

The assertive leader must also be an honest and honest person. The team needs to perceive him as someone who is coherent and trustworthy. This is the basis for decisions to have an impact and credibility on employees. From this, the commitment to the actions they must take is built.

It is also important for this type of leader to have a high sense of responsibility. This not only has to do with carrying out the activities and tasks specific to the work, but it also includes responsibility for each and every one of the people you lead. In other words, it must be able to respond to the expectations that others place on it and commit to the growth of its leaders.

The Decalogue of the Assertive Leader

The abilities of the assertive leader can be summarized in a decalogue. This can be of great help if you hold a leadership position and want assertiveness to be your axis:

1. The assertive leader has clear objectives and seeks to ensure that they benefit the

entire team.

2. It knows how to identify and recognize the strengths and weaknesses of its leaders.

3. He is firm when it comes to making decisions.

4. It communicates openly and honestly.

5. It provides its guidelines in a clear and concise manner.

6. Stay calm and approachable.

7. It offers respectful, helpful, and honest feedback.

8. It promotes collaboration.

9. He has excellent interpersonal relationships with his team members.

10. Lead by example.

4.2 How to exercise authority assertively

"There is no authority such as that which is based on justice and is exercised by virtue." -Pliny the Younger-

Authority is a complex concept, which not everyone understands. It is present in all kinds of hierarchical relationships such as those between parents and children, teachers and students, government officials and the governed, and, of course, leaders and work teams. When it is not exercised properly, it is often a source of friction, tension and conflict.

Authority is defined as the power to rule over other people who are subordinate. It is effective when such subordinates follow orders out of conviction and with a sense of commitment. It is ineffective if compliance is only formal. In the latter case, the person obeys his external behavior, but internally he does not feel respect, nor does he give credibility or legitimacy to the person who issues the order. For the same reason, in the act of complying there is no commitment, much less interest.

It could be said that in most cases orders that are not carried out, or half-fulfilled, speak of ill-exercised authority. Rather than a sanction or a wake-up call for those who disobey, it should invite reflection for those who give the order.

Frequent errors in the exercise of authority

In most cases, authority is rejected because it is perceived as arbitrary, irrational, or inconsistent. This usually happens when the leader gives whimsical or incomprehensible orders. Also when it imposes excessive or impractical burdens on its subordinates, without taking into account the impact this causes on them.

Likewise, it is possible that the relationship is tense and that orders may be perceived as retaliation or manifestations of a latent conflict. For someone to comply, they must be aware of the usefulness of the order and of the reasons why it is imperative to obey it.

The main mistakes of leaders in the field of authority are the following:

- Inconsistency. The answer to contempt is not always the same. Sometimes it is let go, other times it is censored. This creates confusion and undermines legitimacy.

- Communication. Sometimes the reason why it is important to fulfill a certain obligation or task is not sufficiently explained.

- Lack of respect. Issuing an order may employ an authoritarian or even rude attitude towards the other person. This sows the seed to be fulfilled out of fear and doing just what is necessary.

- Lack of empathy. The other person's condition or condition is not taken into account. If you have a lot of work or don't have the tools to do what is asked of you, complying is going to be very difficult.

- Authoritarianism. Leaders who use their power in an authoritarian way are generally not respected, but rather feared. This refusal may be expressed in total or partial breaches of your orders.

- Reinforcement. Sometimes, and usually without noticing it, contempt is re-warded. A member of the team can make a profit by being rebellious, when too much attention is given or causes confusion in the leader.

In this regard, it should be noted that people are not robots. Therefore, you should not expect that in all situations they will meet any requirement, one hundred percent. There should be a small margin for flexibility, without this meaning condescension.

The keys to assertive authority

To exercise assertive authority, there are two pillars: empathy and good communication. Both aspects are decisive if you want to achieve a genuine commitment on the part of your work team. Empathy prevents you from acting arbitrarily; good communication facilitates compliance and allows you to redirect a decision, if necessary.

Other keys to exercising assertive authority are the following.

Establish clear boundaries

It's important for your team to be very clear about where the red lines are. These are rules, orders or conduct that for no reason can they violate, under penalty of any sanction. Of course, you have to be very consistent in this: you can't make exceptions.

The ideal is that every time you give an order or entrust a task, you establish or remember what the non-negotiable aspects are. Assertive authority is exercised consistently, or it is not exercised.

Disaggregate appropriately

You don't want to give a lot of orders at the same time. Try to take adequate time to explain what you want the other person to do and how they should do it. Make sure that your collaborator understands both what they should do and why they should do it.

With regard to regulations, it is common for an organization to issue regulations and with this it is taken for granted that everything is already understood. It is advisable to discuss the most relevant regulations with new workers and verify that they understand the meaning of them.

Coherence and compliance

There must be perfect harmony between what is said and done, in all areas. As we noted before, the best way to lead is by example. So the best thing is to make sure that you fully comply with what you enact. This will make your word valuable in the eyes of your collaborators.

This applies especially to what you announce or promise. If you tell your team that there will be a promotion to new positions, you must comply. If not, you'd better not say anything. If you tell them that a fault will have consequences, you should also make sure that's the case.

Non-verbal language

It is important that nonverbal language is consistent with an assertive communication style. The best thing to do is to use a calm tone of voice. Never give orders out loud, or do it as if you were begging for a favor. Look into the eyes of your interlocutor and show a gesture of openness.

Listener

For the assertive communication process to be genuine, you must not take for granted what the other party has to say. If you give an order, in addition to making sure that it is understood, ask if the person considers it important to do what is instructed, and if they have any suggestions or concerns. In the same way, if things don't go as expected, listen to what the other person has to say before making decisions.

4.3 How to Delegate Tasks Effectively

"The best executive is one who has enough judgment to choose good collaborators to do what needs to be done, and enough restraint not to meddle while they do it." -Theodore Roosevelt-

Delegating is the act of reassigning tasks and responsibilities to other members of the team. Knowing why, when and how to do it is a great advantage for an assertive leader. If you do it efficiently, you increase productivity, improve the skills of your collaborators and allow your team to develop new strengths.

In general, it is delegated to redistribute responsibilities in a more equitable way, to take advantage of the strengths of one of the team members or to develop the potential of collaborators. It is a way to build trust and reinforce leadership. It is a process that requires order and coherence in order to succeed.

Delegation is usually a powerful encouragement for the members of the work team. It also makes it possible to lighten the leader's workload and becomes a vehicle for promotion that reinforces horizontal relationships while maintaining authority.

When do you need to delegate?

The first thing you should be clear about is that there is a big difference between assigning tasks and delegating tasks. Referring someone to do a certain activity does not mean delegating it to them. Delegation involves taking on new responsibilities, part of which belong to the leader. As a result, this worker will have more autonomy in some regard and will raise their status within the team.

Many leaders are not sure what is the ideal time or situation to delegate. There's an easy way to find out. Although it is not an infallible method, a good option is to answer a series of questions with "yes" or "no". The questions must be answered by the leader and are as follows:

1. Do you usually take work home or do you have to do it outside normal hours?

2. Do you tend to disavow your subordinates?

3. Do you take on tasks that your team can cover?

4. Is it common for you to accumulate pending tasks?

5. Do you sometimes have to set aside fundamental tasks to supervise the work of your team?

6. Are you sympathetic to the mistakes of your collaborators?

7. Have you verified that your equipment works properly when there is no supervision?

8. If you were incapacitated, do you think any member of your team could assume your duties?

9. Do your collaborators frequently propose initiatives to you?

10. Is it common for your organization to delegate part of management tasks?

Score one point for every "yes" you answered in the first five questions and one point for every "no" you answered in the last five. If the total sum is more than 5, you should start thinking about delegating tasks.

What tasks can you delegate?

This is another of the questions that come up with leaders when they are in the delegation process: which activities should be delegated and which are not? Not all tasks or responsibilities are fit to be left in the hands of another person. In general terms, it is not possible to entrust anyone with those activities in which only you can add a differential value.

The tasks to be delegated usually fall into one of the following categories:

- Tasks that will be repeated in the future. Recurrent tasks, which are sufficiently standardized, can usually be delegated without any problem.

- Tasks that match the strengths of a team member. If one of the members of the team has significant potential for any of the tasks, has special training in it or has expressed interest and aptitude to carry it out, the best thing is to delegate it to him.

- Tasks associated with the objectives of a team member. As in the previous case, if the task coincides with the professional objectives of one of the collaborators, it is worth taking on it.

- Partial supervisory tasks. If a person has been in a position for a long time, it is very likely that they are quite familiar with the process and the expected results.

You could delegate part of the supervision of the activity to him.

How to Delegate Effectively

For the delegation process to be done effectively, it is best to carry it out in an organized and structured manner. How to do it? You just need to complete the following steps.

Step 1. Define the objective

Once you have verified if the delegation is really appropriate, the next thing is to establish a clear objective. What do you expect from the performance of the team member to whom you are going to delegate? Define it in one sentence and communicate it to the chosen person.

Ideally, you should also need between three and five specific objectives. This will then allow you to follow up more closely.

Step 2. Provides context and guidance

You must ensure that the person you choose has all the information necessary to enable them to carry out their work successfully. This includes things such as:

- Product that you must deliver.

- How you should do the work.

- Delivery dates.

- Tools needed to do the job.

- Desired result.

In the same way, you need to clarify some crucial aspects about the context. For example, goals associated with the work of the team in general; degree of priority of the task; people involved in the activity to be carried out, etc. If you dedicate a little time to this step, it will save you a lot of inconvenience.

Step 3. Follow up

Delegating a task and giving the appropriate instructions does not mean completely forgetting about the matter. The best thing is to define an agenda of meetings with the chosen person, so that both of you can verify that the activity is taking place, based on what was agreed.

Step 4. Measure results

If you have defined the objectives in an appropriate way, this step will be very simple for you. You just have to compare the worker's performance with these objectives. Have they been fulfilled or not? If not, review with your collaborator the possible reasons why this has happened.

Step 5. Recognize the work and provide feedback

Once your collaborator completes the delegated task, it's very important that you recognize their effort and achievement. Also, give him some additional indications or observations regarding his performance. If the results obtained are satisfactory, you can give it more autonomy in the future, always without stopping doing basic checks.

4.4 How to manage conflict situations in the work environment

"Concord makes small things grow, discord ruins big things." -Sallust-

Conflicts are one of the most challenging aspects of assertive leadership. If properly managed, they usually represent a great opportunity for everyone involved to grow and develop. If not handled correctly, they can become a breaking point for the team and for the leader.

Conflict is spoken of when one or more people have interests, needs or desires that contradict those of another or other people. This results in a confrontation that can be direct or camouflaged.

In such cases, the assertive leader must act as a mediator between the parties. It is also advisable to take advantage of the situation to get the whole team to move forward in some aspect. How to do it? What should be considered? We'll talk about this right away.

Main causes of the conflict

It is normal for there to be conflicts within the framework of work, from time to time. In fact, it's also healthy. You should only be concerned if these are very frequent or have a very high intensity. If so, it's best to thoroughly examine the situation.

In general, conflicts at work are caused by one or more of the following causes:

- Scarcity of resources. If equipment or work items are scarce, there may be some tension, because you must compete for those resources.

- Poor distribution of tasks. Some of the team members may feel that their workload is greater than that of their colleagues; or that they are doing activities that other people should do.

- Different work styles. In common activities, there may be two people with very different ways of working. For example, one of them is excessively tidy, while the other is a little more careless.

- Increased pressure. At times when there is increased pressure, such as close to delivery dates, susceptibility and intolerance are also more likely to increase.

- Different interests. When there is contradiction in interests, there is also more likely to be conflict. For example, one of the collaborators may be focused on being very punctual with the delivery date, while the other seeks to improve the product, even if this means asking for a new deadline.

- Values found. Political, religious and even sporting differences sometimes give rise to strong tensions.

- Poor communication. Sometimes the conflict is the result of misunderstandings or errors in the interpretation of the messages.

Types of conflict

To resolve conflicts in a successful way, it's important to understand that not everyone is the same. Just as they have different causes, they can also involve several actors, or be of a very different nature. They are usually classified into three groups.

Depending on the nature of the conflict

In this case, the source of the conflict is taken into account. From that point of view, we found the following:

- False. When there is no real contradiction, but rather a misunderstanding or misperception occurs.

- True. If there is a real contradiction between interests, values, interpretations or perceptions.

- Contingent. It is a temporary conflict that originates in a very specific situation, which is temporary.

- Displaced. The apparent reason for the conflict is not real, but rather it conceals a much greater contradiction.

- Poorly attributed. If it is repressed, hidden or there is not even awareness that it exists.

According to the causes that motivate the conflict

From the point of view of causes, we find five types of conflict:

- Of relationship. When the cause is the clash of two personalities that are very different.

- Of communication. If the cause is a lack of information or a misunderstanding.

- Of interest. When each of the stakeholders defends their own interests and hinders those of others.

- Structural. It occurs when there is a deep cultural or educational clash between two or more people.

- Of values. If the conflict originates from the contradiction of values.

According to the parties involved

In this case, we take into account the people who are participating or are involved in a conflict. From that point of view, there are the following types:

- Intrapersonal. When the conflict is present only in one person, without directly involving others, but generating tension.

- Interpersonal. If the conflict involves two or more people.

- Intragroup. It occurs when the whole group as a whole participates in the conflict, in one way or another.

- Intergroup. If it occurs between two groups of people.

- Inter-organizational. When the conflict occurs between two or more organizations.

How to manage conflict

The golden rule for managing a conflict well is to deal with it as quickly as possible, so that it has no chance to grow or worsen. If you have good communication with your team, those conflicting situations will most likely not go unnoticed by you. As soon as you detect tension and friction, take action.

Other aspects to consider are the following.

Study the situation

Once you detect a conflict, the best thing is to gather as much information as possible about it. Talk to your team members one-on-one, informally. It tries to obtain two pieces of information in particular: who is involved in the conflict and what is the general cause. Then, analyze what type of conflict it is.

Listen to the parties involved

When you have a more or less complete idea of what's going on, it's time to take the second step. This consists of listening to the people involved in the problem. In these situations, more than in any other, it is convenient to use the tools of active listening. This will allow you to understand not only what's happening, but how the people on your team feel about it.

Define a goal

If you have a clear picture and you already know the versions of each of the parts, you have the tools to make way for solutions. For this, first of all, define a goal. What do you hope or want to achieve with the conflict resolution process? Try to be very precise when answering.

You need strategies

Once the objective is defined, think about the strategy that could be most effective in each specific case. Do you need to bring both parties together to come to an agreement? Is it better to talk to each one separately? Is it only necessary to talk to one of the parties? Should the situation be shared with the whole team?

There are some techniques you can use to resolve the conflict:

- Arbitration. It consists of having you propose the solution to the problem yourself. It usually doesn't work well.

- Facilitation. It has to do with making it possible for the parties to talk to lower the tension. Sometimes it's enough to resolve a conflict.

- Mediation. It's a facilitation moderated by you, in all aspects. In this case, we are not only looking for relaxation, but also for a solution-oriented decision.

- Inquiry. It consists of consulting other members of the team or experts to recommend possible solutions.

- Negotiation. It is the process by which differences are recognized and solutions are proposed in which both must give way, but also both must gain something.

You need solutions

Ideally, the parties to the conflict should propose possible solutions. However, as a leader you also need to have your own idea about it. Sometimes management decisions need to be made to resolve the problem. For example, moving one of the collaborators to another section or defining schedules for the use of the tools, etc.

Follow up

It is necessary to closely monitor the conflict situation, once a solution has been agreed upon. It may be detected that the output is not sufficient and then it will need to be adjusted. It is also possible that everything will be solved. In any case, it is impossible to verify one or the other if the subject is not kept under observation.

4.5 Motivating teams and a positive work environment: Practical tips

"Aim for the moon. If you fail, you could give it a star." -William Clement Stone-

An assertive leader knows that motivation is one of the axes of good performance at work. For this reason, it spares no effort in the task of positively influencing employees so that they do their best and, at the same time, feel that the organization corresponds in the same way.

Motivation is much more than a flashy speech. It has to do with making value propositions to employees, so that they feel that it is worth fully committing to their tasks and to the organization. It is not only motivated by offering tangible benefits, but also by creating an achievement-oriented corporate culture. How to do it? Why is it necessary? Let's see.

Tips for motivating and creating a positive environment

A charismatic leader can make memorable interventions by motivating his collaborators. Surely, they will leave the meeting with the firm intention of being better. However, no matter how inspiring the leader is, it is likely that after a few days there will be very little left of the enthusiasm he generated with his speech.

Employees need concrete and continuous incentives to experience real motivation in relation to their activities and to the organization. A speech is not enough, even if it's brilliant. There are elements that are more present in the worker's daily life and that will be definitive in motivating them. The most relevant are the following.

An attractive work environment

The work environment includes both the material context and the work environment. As for the former, the ideal is that each worker has the necessary tools to do their job well and that they are in good condition. Also that the facilities are comfortable. It is not necessary to have luxuries, but there are basic conditions for performance to be the most adequate.

The work environment has to do with corporate culture. If kindness and good manners prevail in the environment, all workers will value the organization more and, consequently, will feel more committed to it. Aspects such as having water or coffee available are usually a small investment, which has great value for employees. Similar stimuli are much appreciated.

A competitive salary

The maxim of "It's not all money" should be thought out and applied in a reasonable way. Earning a good salary is motivating for any worker. In fact, it doesn't have to be higher than average, but it doesn't have to be lower either. In the latter case, it becomes a factor of demotivation.

The concept of "emotional salary" must also be taken into account. This includes the non-economic remuneration that workers receive and that improve their quality of life.

For example, the working day may be slightly shorter. Or maybe it's possible to give one day off per month. Similar benefits make up for a salary that isn't particularly attractive.

Flexibility and reconciliation

All workers value autonomy very much. One of the aspects in which this materializes is the flexibility of schedules. The ideal is to work for objectives and not for strict deadlines, if the work activity allows it. Therefore, if a person finishes their work early, they may well go home even if it is not the usual time of departure.

An organization that is open to the needs of its workers is much more valued by them. The best thing is to leave a door open so that employees can negotiate some benefits in their favor, such as arriving later, leaving earlier or having a four-day work week. This will make them feel more committed to the company.

Empathetic leadership

One of the basic functions of a leader is to motivate his team. The best way to do this is to become a guide and an ally for your collaborators. When they see in him someone who manages to establish common objectives and reconcile them with individual objectives, a lasting balance is generated.

A good manager is often all that is needed to make the worker feel that they are in the right place. And so that, based on this, he personally commits himself to the smooth running of the organization.

Allow the team to set rewards

It's not easy to generalize what different people perceive as rewards. Likewise, teams are often quite diverse (in age, educational level, etc.) and that is why it is not easy to determine which incentives have the most impact on them.

A good idea is to allow the same team to set up a rewards plan. They must define when and how to apply it, as well as the benefit to be obtained. No one better than themselves to decide all this. In addition, leaving this matter in their hands is a gesture of trust that they will also value.

Recognition and feedback

A worker will feel much more motivated when they see that their work does not go unnoticed by the organization's leaders. Even this was proven by the famous psychologist Elton Mayo, through a study known as the "Hawthorne Experiment" (1932).

That study found that workers significantly improved their performance when they were carefully supervised and their needs were noted. Likewise, when they obtained feedback from their superiors regarding the work they were doing. In other words: "invisible" workers don't feel motivated.

Career Development Options

Investing in the well-being of workers is a very powerful incentive. One way to do this is by offering training for continuous improvement. This allows a person to grow and that evolution generates great satisfaction.

In the same way, it is important for a person to feel that within their organization they have opportunities to move up. The expectation of a better position, a better salary and greater autonomy are high-impact motivations for any employee.

4.6 Practical exercises to improve leadership skills

Next, we propose a series of exercises for you to develop your leadership skills. It goes without saying that all assertive skills are acquired and, therefore, require training in order for them to emerge and increase.

Observation exercise

Think of a leader who inspires you and look for one of his public or private speeches on video. Take a good look at three aspects: what kind of language do you use? What is your non-verbal language like? What elements make you an inspirational leader?

Then, do the same activity, but this time look for a video of a leader who seems unfriendly or uncharismatic to you. Analyze their verbal and non-verbal language, as well as the elements that generate rejection in this person.

What would you do if...?

This is an exercise that can help you become aware of your attitudes towards the work team and also to predict possible answers. The first thing is to make a list of the most uncomfortable situations you can imagine within your work team. For example, if one of your collaborators is rude, yells at you, or refuses to follow your orders. Think about extreme situations.

What follows is to answer the question "What would you do if (each of these situations occurs)?" Think about what you would feel at that moment and what would be the most assertive response in that scenario.

Conflict resolution

For a week, observe your work team to identify five of the conflicts you detect in one or more members of the group. Define each conflict in a single sentence. Then, think of three possible solutions to that problem.

The first should be as conventional a solution as possible. The second is a solution that is as assertive as possible. The third, a disruptive solution, the most original thing you can imagine. Try to project yourself and think about what the effects of each of the solutions would be.

Non-verbal language

Record on video at least three meetings you have with your team. Then, take a closer look at how you made use of body language. Observe the gestures that appear on your face, the posture of your body, the movement of your hands and feet, and the position of your head.

Indicate whether each of the gestures and body movements correspond to: 1) An aggressive, intimidating or authoritarian attitude; 2) A nervous, shy or shy attitude; 3) A neutral, distant or cold attitude; 4) A sympathetic, affable, fun attitude; 5) Other attitudes. Finally, analyze everything and draw a conclusion about the use of your non-verbal language.

Assertive language

Take a piece of paper and draw three to five geometric figures. Ask someone you trust to also pick up a pen and paper. Tell that person what to draw, without mentioning the name of the figure you drew. In the end, notice what the person did on the paper. It will give you a very clear idea about how precise you are with language.

Conclusion

In this chapter we have seen how assertiveness can be applied to a field as relevant as leadership. It's important to note that you don't have to be a business leader to put what you've seen into practice. The knowledge acquired can also be applied to situations such as teaching, raising children, managing family situations, etc.

Whatever the case, don't lose sight of the following points:

- The assertive leader is characterized by self-confidence. This is reflected in other aspects, such as assertive communication, empathy, honesty and responsibility.

- Assertive authority is based on empathy and good communication. To exercise it, it is necessary to establish clear limits, explain what you are looking for, be coherent, listen actively and comply with the word.

- Delegating is sharing responsibilities with another person. To do this effectively, you must choose what is delegated, to whom and at what time. Likewise, define objectives, provide context and guidance, monitor, measure results and provide recognition.

- Conflict can be of several types and originate from different causes. It must be addressed quickly, listening to the parties, defining objectives, creating solution strategies and following up on the situation.

- Motivation is essential to increase productivity. Some of the most motivating factors are the work environment, salary, flexibility, empathy and professional development options, among others.

In the next chapter we are going to talk about one of the decisive issues in the development of assertiveness: self-esteem. We will learn about their importance and different tactics and strategies to increase security and self-love. You can't miss it because it will be very useful for you. See you!

CHAPTER 5: RAISING SELF-ESTEEM TO THE MAXIMUM

"Have faith in what exists in there." -André Gide-

Who is considered the most successful president in the history of the United States? Abraham Lincoln, the same one to whom Walt Whitman dedicated the famous poem "Oh Captain, My Captain". Did you know that Lincoln never had access to a school? That's right. He became an extraordinary self-taught person.

But the most interesting thing in his life is not that. Abraham Lincoln failed in business when he was just 31 years old. At 32, he suffered his first defeat at the polls. At 34 he was completely ruined. At 35, he lost the one he loved most: his wife. At 36, he suffered a nervous breakdown. At 37, he recovered, but failed again in the elections at 38 and 43.

He only won his first electoral victory at the age of 46. However, he went through new electoral defeats at 48, 55, 56 and 58. Despite everything, at 60 he became the 16th president of the United States and one of the most famous leaders of all time. Abraham Lincoln is a model of what it means to have faith in oneself, not to depend on external events and to persevere to achieve goals.

In this chapter we are going to address the topic of self-esteem. We will talk about its importance, the mental obstacles to developing it and the most effective techniques and strategies to overcome fears, insecurity and learn to believe in oneself.

5.1 The importance of self-esteem in assertive communication

"Never lower your head. Always keep it very high. He looks the world right in the eye." -Helen Keller-

Self-esteem is closely related to assertiveness. Self-love is necessary to develop a communication in which respect for oneself and for the other prevails. If there is no appreciation for oneself, either inhibition or a desire to impose oneself on others appears.

Self-esteem refers to the vision that each person has of themselves. This, in turn, depends on how you judge yourself and results in some level of satisfaction or dissatisfaction with what you are. All of this is reflected in attitude and behavior, which includes the way we communicate.

The relationship between self-esteem and assertiveness

Both self-esteem and assertiveness are two pillars of emotional intelligence. If a person considers himself to be someone valuable and worthy of love, regardless of his faults or the mistakes he may make, he will reflect this well-being in his relationship with other people.

When someone accepts and respects themselves, they have no problem expressing their wants and needs in a frank and direct way, without fear of rejection from others. Likewise, it will not tolerate abuse or contempt, but will demand dignified treatment. In other words, you'll be able to communicate assertively.

It is often believed that some people have an aggressive communication style because their self-esteem is too high. However, this is not true. What happens in these cases is that the person has built a wall between them and the world to hide their feelings of vulnerability and incompetence.

People with a passive communication style also have little appreciation for themselves, to the point where they are able to put the rights of others before their own. They behave defensively, as if they don't want to bother anyone, because they are very afraid of rejection or abandonment.

From all this, a fundamental premise emerges: if a person has high self-esteem, they can communicate assertively. And, at the same time, if the person regularly communicates in an assertive manner, it will raise their self-esteem.

Where to start?

Although self-esteem and assertive communication are mutually reinforcing, it's not really possible to be assertive if you don't have confidence in yourself. So, if you're wondering: what should I work on first? , the answer is: self-esteem.

If self-love is not solid, no matter how hard you try to be assertive in your communication, sooner or later you will engage in aggressive or passive behavior, even without realizing it. The basis of everything is to have a good relationship with yourself, because otherwise you won't have a good relationship with others.

Now, how to increase self-esteem? It is very important to work on emotional barriers and the development of positive coping skills. Also about fears and insecurities. We will talk about all these topics below.

5.2 Identifying and Overcoming Emotional Barriers

"Nothing is as serious as it seems when you think about it." -Daniel Kahneman-

Emotional barriers are obstacles that we place on ourselves, almost always unconsciously, and that hinder or prevent the achievement of our goals. They also prevent an adequate discernment of reality. It could be said that they are a form of self-sabotage, which we don't usually notice.

If you don't fight against emotional barriers, they can have a profound impact on your life. In general, they don't let you move forward smoothly and that's why they tend to be the prelude to frustration. But, in addition, if you let yourself be invaded by them, they can lead to serious problems such as depression or anxiety.

How to detect emotional barriers

As we already noted, emotional barriers are usually unconscious. Because of this, you don't always realize that they are present in your life. They seep into your behavior and camouflage themselves behind attitudes such as prudence, good manners or seriousness.

However, there are some behaviors that talk about the presence of these barriers. Some of them are the following:

- Extreme shyness.

- Feelings of envy or distrust of others, which are very recurrent.

- Nervousness during social interactions

- Tendency to judge others extremely harshly

- Extreme fear of rejection or lack of acceptance.

- Lack of ongoing motivation.

- Constant pessimism.

- Inability to visualize solutions.

- Don't act out of fear of failure.

- Don't attend social gatherings out of fear of rejection.

If you have one or more of these behaviors, you are most likely carrying emotional barriers that you haven't become aware of.

Causes

Emotional barriers are born and consolidated for a variety of reasons. In principle, they are due to internal causes such as fear, insecurity and a feeling of inferiority. This may be the result of inappropriate or abusive parenting, or the result of living in a highly competitive or disrespectful environment.

Sometimes emotional barriers are temporary or circumstantial, that is, they are not permanent, but appear in a specific life situation. In that case, they are most likely caused by high levels of stress or anxiety.

These obstacles can also be the result of a negative social atmosphere. There are groups or societies that turn out to be very exclusive or persecutory and this may activate emotional barriers. For example, when an immigrant arrives in a country where they are not well received.

From the point of view of Eastern philosophies, the origin of these types of barriers lies in attachment. People are unable to move forward because they hold on to ideas, feelings, people, situations, beliefs, past events, etc. This leads to blocking their development.

How to overcome emotional barriers?

Now that we are clear about what emotional barriers are and what their possible causes are, we must move on to the important thing: overcoming them. To do so, let's ask ourselves: what are these obstacles made up of? The answer is: from negative thoughts. Each one of those thoughts is like a brick that ends up forming that wall that doesn't let you evolve.

Negative thoughts routinely filter into your mind. They're rude and that's why you don't realize that they're there, giving you orders about what you should think and how you should act. Sometimes they appear as clearly negative statements such as: "I won't be able to", "I can't stand out", "I don't stand out", "No one likes me", "I'm an idiot", "I always do everything wrong", etc. Other times they arise accompanied by discomfort or apparent laziness: "Why do it?" , "I'm not in the mood", "The result will always be the same", "I'll be bored", etc.

Everything together predisposes you to, in effect, what is in your mind coming true. If you think you're not going to be able to, you probably can't because you're taking away your will and energy from the start to achieve it. If you think that you are going to be rejected, without realizing it you will adopt defensive and suspicious attitudes, which will not have a positive response from others.

Thus, the way to combat negative thoughts, which are the components of emotional barriers, is to detect them and replace them with positive thoughts. It's much easier said than done, but it's not as difficult as you might imagine.

The key to everything is to start with small things. If you don't have confidence in yourself, it's not enough to say, "Yes, I can do it." Statements like that will only contradict your most deeply held beliefs, and you won't give them credit yourself. So it's best to start with simple things. For example, try to detect the best thing about a space in which you are. Or look for a virtue in the people around you. Or, perhaps, stop for a moment to see the beauty of a tree or the sky.

Go step by step, being a hunter of virtues in everything that surrounds you, including people, animals and things. You will see how this affects the way you see the world and will end up making you more aware of the way you see yourself. In this way, negative thoughts will not go unnoticed, but you will be able to capture and nuance them or eliminate them. If you practice meditation, this process will be much easier for you.

5.3 Developing positive coping skills

"For some reason, once we faced them, we found that our own demons are not what we imagined." -Nelson DeMille-

Another key to increasing self-esteem and promoting assertive communication is the development of positive coping skills. As you know, pain and difficulty are inevitable realities in anyone's life. What you can choose is how you respond to this.

Positive coping skills are intentional mental response schemes. They are aimed at managing internal and external demands, as well as conflicts that may arise between them, and which have one characteristic: they apparently exceed the psychological resources you have to respond.

In other words, these skills allow you to respond to the demands you make of yourself, or that other people make of you, in such a way that you can tolerate, reduce, minimize or dominate the situation. This would be a positive coping. However, you can also flee, destroy, give up, etc. In this case, we are talking about negative coping. Let's look at this in more detail.

Coping

Coping is defined as "a set of cognitive and behavioral strategies that the person uses to manage internal or external demands that are perceived as excessive for the individual's resources" (Lazarus and Folkman 1984).

The ability to deal with a situation of this type not only includes the ability to give it a practical solution, but it also involves the proper management of the emotions associated with this stressful situation. In the face of such an event, people make two types of evaluations:

- Primary assessment. It consists of identifying if the situation is positive, negative or neutral. Also estimate the possible immediate consequences of the event and the future ones. On that basis, it is established how demanding or challenging the event is.

- Secondary assessment. In this case, the resources or capacities that one has to deal with that situation are analyzed. In other words, how fit we feel to successfully overcome the event. This type of assessment is what generates stress.

From this, we draw the conclusion that we want to make clear in this section: the stress of a situation does not depend on the situation itself, but on the assessment we make of it.

Factors that influence the assessment of the facts

Two people may face the same challenge and each of them perceives it very differently and, consequently, responds differently. What does this depend on? There are a few factors that set the contrast:

- Self-esteem. The higher the self-esteem, the lower the stress in the face of challenging situations and vice versa.

- Ability to take risks. Some people are stimulated by challenges, while others are intimidated by them.

- A sense of competition. The more self-control a person has, the less stress they experience.

- Optimism. It's the hope that everything will work out. It is associated with the above variables.

- Adaptability. People who adapt more easily to change tend to feel less overwhelmed by challenging situations.

- Communication capacity. If a person knows how to communicate well, they will feel more secure when it comes to facing challenges.

- Social support. People who feel protected and valued by their environment also experience more self-confidence when facing challenges.

Coping strategies

Coping strategies are practices that are carried out to manage a stressful situation. Such practices can be positive or negative. The former correspond to an appropriate approach to the situation and allow maintaining or regaining control over the situation. The latter assume the opposite.

- Positive coping strategies cover three aspects:

- The assessment of the critical event. It has to do with finding meaning in the situation.

- The problem. It corresponds to the identification of the difficulty required by an approach.

- Emotion. It refers to the emotions involved in the critical event.

Based on the above, we talk about three types of strategies:

- Problem-focused strategies. It corresponds to coping strategies in which emotions are controlled and, therefore, it is possible to focus on solving the problem.

- Strategies focused on emotions. In this case, the emphasis should be placed on emotions, since they are out of control. The goal is to calm down or relax.

- Strategies focused on avoidance. It refers to situations that it is preferable to avoid for the time being, in order to gather resources to deal with them.

Positive Coping Techniques

There are several positive coping techniques. Depending on the type of situation you face, you can choose one or the other. It is also possible to use several at the same time. The main ones are the following:

Acceptance

It means recognizing the problem and allowing it to continue as it is, without pretending that things are different, and adapting to the situation. For example: the lockdown caused by the Covid 19 pandemic. There was no alternative but to adapt to restrictions.

Escape or avoidance

It occurs when the situation exceeds a person's psychological tools to cope with it. For example, when someone uses yelling and insulting words to you. Before reacting, you prefer to step away from the situation for a moment in order to balance yourself and be able to respond calmly to that aggression.

Self-analysis

It involves the recognition of one's own emotions and of the responsibilities one has in the development of a problem. It means focusing our gaze inward on oneself to organize ideas and emotions. Like when someone makes a complaint to you and before answering them, you analyze whether they may be right, thus facilitating understanding.

Positive reevaluation

It consists of looking for a new perspective to see the problem. On the one hand, trying not to dramatize it, nor to highlight the most difficult aspects. On the other hand, trying to find either positive aspects, or ways to make some use of the negative situation. For example, a person is fired from their job and, instead of focusing on the loss, tries to see it as an opportunity to make some change in their life.

Catharsis

In this coping technique, the aim is to express all negative feelings, without affecting anyone or hurting themselves. A clear example of this is keeping a diary in which those emotions are recorded. In doing so, there is a sense of liberation and emotions become less intense.

Request help

It has to do with specifying in what specific aspects help is required and seeking it effectively to solve the problem. An example would be that of a person who has been scammed and seeks the services of a lawyer to indicate the route to follow.

5.4 How to overcome fears and insecurity

"Love drives away fear and, conversely, fear drives love away. And not only does fear drive out love, but also intelligence, goodness, all thoughts of beauty and truth, and only silent desperation remains; and in the end, fear comes to expel humanity itself from man". -Aldous Huxley-

In principle, fear is a very positive emotion. It is a reaction to a real danger and is related to the instinct for survival. A person who lacks fear would jump onto a highway full of cars at full speed, or jump into an abyss without precautions. It probably wouldn't last long alive.

Thus, fear is part of the survival team of all mammals and its function is protective. Now, the problem is when you start to feel it, without there actually being a threat or danger to your life or your integrity. Even more problematic, if it is an almost constant emotion. Let's see why this is happening.

The nature of fear

Fear is a basic, primary and universal emotion. It is a defense mechanism that is activated when there is a threat, that is, some factor that can put integrity or life at risk, without us being able to do anything about it. In other words, there are two components to fear: the threat as such and the perception that the resources to deal with it are scarce or insufficient.

That said, there is also a modality known as "dysfunctional fear". This is the one that takes place when there is no real danger, but fear still breaks out. Previously, this was called "fear without an object", but it is more accurate to say that it is a "fear with an internal object"; that is, that what we fear only exists within ourselves.

Dysfunctional fear can lead to anxiety, when it becomes more imprecise and continuous. Some people are more likely to experience this type of fear when they have traits such as:

- Low self-esteem or unstable self-esteem

- Confusing self-concept.

- Lack of self-confidence.

- Pessimism.

Insecurity is a manifestation of fear. It usually has to do with other fears such as fear of rejection, abandonment or failure. Is there a way to overcome this situation? Of course it is. We'll talk about this right away.

Tips for overcoming fear and insecurity

The golden rule for overcoming fear and insecurity is to face them. In reality, there is no other way to solve this problem. However, there are several ways to deal with these fears. The following are the most effective.

Name your fear

Dysfunctional fear is often rather inaccurate. It is as if you are afraid of everything and at the same time of nothing. A good option is to keep a fear diary for three or four weeks. Record when fear appears, when it intensifies and how you experience it. Ideally, you should be able to put a name to that fear, even if it's not that exact. For example: "I am afraid of the dark because I feel that there can be many threats hidden within it, which I cannot grasp."

Accept it

You may spend a lot of energy and resources trying to hide your fears. However, most likely, you won't succeed. Instead of hiding them, the right thing to do is to accept that you have them and even talk about them with other people. This will detract from them some of their relevance.

Use your breathing

Breathing is a great ally to increase control over emotions. One of the physiological reactions to fear is agitation of breathing. That's why, if you stop for a moment and try to breathe more deeply, you'll probably feel more calm. Breathe in very vigorously and breathe out with a little less energy.

Use your imagination in a positive way

Fears are fueled by a vivid imagination that sees dangers where there are none and gives omnipotence to real threats. The good thing is that you can also use your imagination to your advantage. At a time when you are calm, think of a situation that frightens you and then draw in your mind an image in which you manage fear perfectly. Even if it seems somewhat childish, you'll find that it helps you a lot.

Get out of your comfort zone

When you step out of your comfort zone and expose yourself to uncertainty, you're taking a big step toward trusting yourself more. Don't miss an opportunity to go to a place you don't know, without a map. Or take a transport route where you don't know where it's going. Any novel experience will have that effect of reducing fears and anxiety.

Motivate yourself through your internal dialogue

Self-talk is one of those factors that can help you increase fear, or reduce it. Persuading yourself that you are capable of dealing with a situation and of overcoming your insecurities will give you greater inner strength. In the same way, reproaching yourself, demanding more from yourself than you can give, or fueling your insecurity will only enhance fears. Try to modify negative thoughts and self-motivate yourself.

Accept that you will fail

One of the most common fears is the fear of failure. However, many people do not stop to think that such failure is an indispensable part of success. Goals are achieved through perseverance, and perseverance involves getting up after falling. You can examine the life of any historical figure and you will find that this is the case. Therefore, do not be discouraged by a failure in order to leave behind fears and insecurities.

Expose yourself to your fear

Exposure is a technique used by psychotherapists to treat very intense phobias and fears. As the name suggests, it has to do with finding what you fear. This is done gradually. The usual thing is to start by imagining the situation that causes fear and then face it using graphics or virtual reality. Then, and only when you're ready, will you expose yourself to the real situation. This is a technique that requires professional support.

Relaxation techniques

Relaxation techniques are very effective in reducing anxiety. The most commonly used are breathing techniques and muscle relaxation techniques. However, there are a whole range of practices you can go to to to feel relaxed more often. For example, mindfulness, yoga, tai chi, etc. All of them can help you a lot in the process of reducing your fears and insecurities.

Learn to live with fear

Fear will always be in your life, one way or another. So your goal should not be to banish any trace of fears, but to learn to live and deal with it. How? Follow the pattern: recognize it, name it, feel it, listen to what it wants to tell you and then let it go.

Ask for help

If you see that your insecurity or your fears do not give way, and you detect that this conditions your life in a significant way, do not hesitate to seek professional help. A psychotherapist can point you the way and help you follow it. Behavioral therapies tend to be more effective in these cases.

5.5 Strategies to increase self-esteem and self-confidence

"Never let anyone tell you that you can't do something. Not even me, okay? If you have a dream, you have to protect it. People who aren't capable of doing something will tell you that you can't either. If you want something, go for it. Period." -Will Smith-

Living without self-love is like living in iron armor. You feel uncomfortable and sore all the time, and you can barely move. Staying still begins to be the least tortuous option and you end up getting used to believing that the world and life are that small space that you inhabit.

Self-esteem gives you that feeling of appreciation and acceptance that you need to trust yourself. In turn, self-confidence allows you to seek new experiences and accept new challenges. When you explore new horizons, you feel more secure. Everything is like a gear in which each piece leads to the others working well.

What happens if you have self-esteem issues?

It's not something definitive, but rather a situation that you can work on. Soon we will give you some keys that will help you improve in this regard.

Strategies to increase self-esteem and self-confidence

There is a principle that is considered the golden rule for increasing self-esteem and self-confidence. He says you shouldn't wait until you feel ready to do something, because chances are you'll never do it. In reality, things happen the other way around: first you do things and then comes the feeling of security. Just act.

In addition to this, there are other strategies you can put into practice to free yourself from the armor of insecurity and lack of self-love. The following are the most important.

Don't pursue self-esteem and security

Although it seems contradictory, the more stubborn you become trying to love yourself more and to feel more confident in what you do, the more difficult it will be for you to achieve that purpose. In this case, a concept known as the "law of invested effort" operates. It points out that excess energy for achievement can have opposite results. Therefore, the best thing is not to obsess, but to keep in mind your goal, understand that you are not going to achieve it quickly, not under all circumstances, and let everything flow.

Start small

The virtuous circle of self-confidence and self-esteem involves the application of the golden rule: act. If two people have an exam and one of them attends but gets a bad grade, they'll still feel better than someone who doesn't attend for fear of failing. The key to all of this is to start with small things. Start with decisions that aren't as compromising and work your way up.

Discover reasons to trust you

If you have low self-esteem, you will most likely tend to underestimate your achievements. It's as if nothing you do is enough to convince you that you are worthy and capable of achieving important goals. You get the idea that if you achieved something it's because it wasn't that difficult or relevant; or that you could have done better. To get that idea out of your head, start by making a list of the three great achievements of your life and identify the abilities or virtues you put into play to achieve them.

Hold on to your values

Values give you extraordinary strength to achieve what you set out to do and, in addition, they strengthen your self-esteem. When you do something, don't focus on the result you get, but on the values that inspire it. Instead of thinking about your exam grade, focus on your desire to improve yourself and the valuable effort you've put into achieving it. In this way, you will be able to give a deeper meaning to what you do.

Reinterpret your fears

Science has shown that the same substance is present in both fear and excitement: adrenaline. This is a component produced by the brain and generates a series of physical and psychological reactions: muscle tension, increased circulatory rate and breathing, etc. It has been proven that if a person interprets their fear as enthusiasm, they can better manage it; this is because both emotions cause the same physiological reactions.

Make decisions

One of the effects of lack of self-esteem and self-confidence is the difficulty in making decisions. The usual thing is that you stay hesitating for a long time or that you postpone the matter and never return to it. That's why it's very important that you start making small decisions, without delay. Start with simple things, always avoiding falling into doubt. Choose something, determine something, evaluating only the basics and not ruminating for hours on what you should do.

Be very honest with yourself

A person who loves himself and trusts in what he is, does not have to hide from the eyes of others, let alone from himself. Being honest is going to help you a lot to accept yourself. Don't be afraid to talk to people you trust about your mistakes, flaws, and fears. Stop thinking that hiding your vulnerabilities will make them disappear. The more sincere you are, with yourself and with others, the greater your self-love and the healthier your interactions with others.

Do things that make you uncomfortable

Getting out of your comfort zone is a key point for increasing your self-esteem and your security. Every time you expand your limits, you also increase your area of action in life. Accepting challenges and exposing yourself to the uncertain will help you a lot. You don't have to set out on a solo trip through an unknown jungle. All you have to do is make progress every day, on small things. Start a conversation with someone strange, take the floor to say something in public, etc.

Avoid the trap of arrogance

Insecurity and lack of self-love can also lead you to act arrogantly. This is not a sign of self-esteem, but rather a mask to hide your fears. So detect and avoid behaviors in which you seek to be above others or brag about something. Remember that assertiveness is characterized by respect for oneself and also for others. This two-track recognition is one of the foundations of mental health.

5.6 Practical exercises to improve self-esteem and overcome insecurities

The following exercises aim to help you allay your insecurities and fears, and, in addition, increase your self-esteem. You can practice them all or choose the ones you feel most comfortable with first. Ideally, you should face these challenges with the conviction that they are a step forward on the path to overcoming you.

Walking with a bandage

This exercise will help you overcome your fears. You just have to put on a blindfold and start walking around your house. Do it slowly and in a space you know well. Focus on the emotions you experience as you move forward. This practice will help you better understand fear and feel more confident in the face of uncertainty.

Discovering labels

It is common for us to be labeled by others, but also for us to put labels on our foreheads ourselves. "The clueless one", "The good people with everyone", "The shy one", etc. This exercise involves you thinking about three of the labels you have given yourself. Identify them and then ask yourself the following:

- When was the first time you thought about that label?

- How does it make you feel?

- What insecurities or fears does it create for you?

Analyze your answers and point out why those labels only define a part of you and not your whole being.

The Honor Board

Make a table with three columns. The first corresponds to praise, the second to abilities and strengths, and the third to self-pride. In the first column, write the five compliments they have given you and that you remember the most; in the second, the five strengths or abilities that you recognize in yourself; in the third, the five aspects that make you feel most proud of yourself.

In the end, analyze what all that data says about you. Finally, keep that table somewhere where you can consult it whenever you feel confused about what you are and what you are worth.

List of awards

Make a list of prizes that you can give to yourself, simply because you appreciate yourself and want to have comforting details that make you feel good. None of the awards should be material and the list should be very long. Take a couple of days to do it. Jot down things like "Listen to 'x' song that I like", or "Prepare a dish that I love", etc.

Then, write down each of these gifts on a piece of paper and store them all in a box that you have intended for this purpose. Every day, at the start of the day, take out one of those pieces of paper and give yourself the prize that is written there.

A Journal of Self-Esteem and Gratitude

The diary is a very effective tool for getting to know you, catharsis and identifying those thought patterns of which you are not very aware. In this case, the recommendation is to make a diary in which you record every night the best thing you did during the day. Also, you should write down a reason to be thankful for; it could be for life, for something you've learned, etc. Check your diary every week and draw conclusions. The best thing to do is to do this for six months.

Conclusion

Throughout this chapter, we have taken a tour of the meaning of self-esteem, the barriers to developing it and the principles and techniques to increase your self-love and gain more confidence in yourself. Keep the following statements in mind:

- Self-esteem is the result of the judgments we make about ourselves and determines the way we behave.

- Self-esteem is closely related to assertiveness. Both are mutually reinforcing.

- Emotional barriers are mental patterns, almost always unconscious, that operate as obstacles to personal growth. They are made up of negative thoughts.

- The key to overcoming emotional barriers is to detect negative thoughts and replace them with positive ones.

- Positive coping is a mental scheme of voluntary and adequate response to stressful or very demanding events.

- The main positive coping techniques are acceptance, escape or avoidance, self-analysis, positive reevaluation, catharsis and asking for help.

- The most effective strategies to overcome fears are: naming them, accepting them, breathing, imagination, leaving the comfort zone, self-motivation, accepting faults, exposure, relaxation, learning to live with fear and asking for help.

- The best strategies to increase self-esteem and psychological safety are to avoid the law of invested effort, start small, discover reasons to trust, hold on to values, reinterpret fears, make decisions, be honest with yourself, do uncomfortable things and avoid arrogance.

We have come to the end of this journey, with the conviction that you will know how to get the most out of it and that it will become a tool for your personal growth and happiness. Let us now move on to the final conclusions.

CONCLUSION

"Who transforms himself transforms the world". -Dalai Lama-

We have finished a journey that we began with the aim of giving you tools so that you can have healthier communication with yourself and with others, so that this will lead you to a fuller life, in which you can be freer and develop all your potential.

The mere fact that you have gone through all these pages has left several seeds sown in your mind. We are sure that you are not the same person you were when you started reading. Now you have more elements to understand yourself and more tools for you to put into practice the art of living. Let's make a final review of what we have learned.

To take note...

It's important to keep in mind that assertive communication is a way to have healthier relationships with yourself and with others. By adopting this communication style, you can ensure that your rights, wishes and needs are respected, without feeling guilty about this, or going over others to achieve it.

If you find it difficult to say "no" to the requirements of others, there are techniques that make it easier for you, such as "the sandwich" and "the fog bank", among others. You just have to familiarize yourself with them and manage your interlocutor's reaction appropriately.

Assertive communication involves the ability to avoid empty speeches, showing clarity and conciseness in everything you express. To achieve this, there is nothing better than thinking before speaking and focusing on the here and now of communication, giving relevance to your interlocutor. Active listening is essential to make all of this possible.

You can become a speaker capable of persuading both a single interlocutor and large and small groups, through principles and behaviors that strengthen self-confidence. Preparing yourself well and applying the right techniques are the way to gain influence and credibility over others. This includes negotiations, where your goal should be to achieve formulas that benefit all parties.

All of the above will allow you to strengthen your leadership skills. Ideally, you should not be an ordinary leader, but someone capable of assertively exercising authority. In this way, you will be able to better motivate others and resolve conflicts, turning them into opportunities for learning and growth for all. It will also help you in the difficult task of sharing responsibilities with the people you manage.

Nothing we have said so far could be put into practice if you don't work to increase your self-esteem and overcome your insecurities. It is not an easy task, but we are convinced that you can achieve it if you insist on doing it. To achieve this, there are several useful strategies, including those aimed at recognizing your worth in a more objective way and promoting practices of self-acceptance and self-care.

How to put into practice what has been learned?

We strongly recommend that you complete all the exercises proposed at the end of each chapter. They are carefully chosen practices so that you develop the competencies and abilities of assertive communication. Some are designed for you to do them only once, while others, such as those associated with avoiding empty speeches, should be done frequently.

The ideal is to set your sights as far as possible: don't be shy in your desires and purposes. At the same time, you must be clear that great achievements are achieved step by step. That's why it's best to start with small daily actions. Don't wait for conditions to be favorable or to "feel ready" to start a change. The right person is you and the right time is now.

Remember that assertive communication and self-esteem are two dimensions that go hand in hand. The higher your self-love, the more assertive your interactions with others will be. And the more assertive those interactions are, the greater your self-esteem. This is a very valuable starting point, which you should not lose sight of.

Start by applying the principles of assertiveness to people with whom you don't have a very close emotional connection. A colleague with whom you speak little, a customer, a salesman, the concierge, in short. Without knowing it, these people will help you increase your skills. Then, apply what you have learned with people who are getting closer and closer. If you succeed, you'll see your social and interpersonal relationships improve a lot.

Public speaking and leading appropriately are very important skills in today's world. Don't miss an opportunity to increase them. Move forward step by step and soon you'll see how far you've come. Motivate yourself and convince yourself that you can achieve it because your greatest weapon is perseverance.

A final tip

Finally, we are going to tell you a Zen story. It talks about a young monk who was training and showed great disposition and intelligence. The time came when he was assigned a wise teacher, who asked him to go out with him to travel the world. After a day on the road, and when it was too late, they arrived at a very poor house and asked its inhabitants to allow them to sleep there.

The family gladly accepted and invited them to drink milk and cheese before going to bed. While they were eating, the hosts told them that they had a cow and that she gave them the sustenance to live. Yes, they were poor, but at least they didn't lack anything to eat, thanks to that animal that asked for little in return.

The teacher and the monk left at dawn to continue their journey. However, the teacher asked the apprentice to take the cow and take it with them. The young man, surprised, did so. When they reached a ravine, the master pushed the animal and threw it into the abyss. The monk didn't know what to say. How was it possible to take the livelihood from that family that had so fondly welcomed them? The teacher made no comment and both went on their way.

After a couple of years, master and apprentice returned to their temple. The monk had learned a lot and now he felt wiser. Anyway, he couldn't forget that episode of the cow, which was so disconcerting for him. So, as soon as he had a chance, he left the temple to look for that family that had hosted them. I wanted to make up for them in some way.

When he arrived at the site, he did not see the humble house that had welcomed them. In its place was an opulent mansion. Despite this, the monk knocked on the door and was very surprised when he saw one of his former hosts open for him. They invited him in and told him what happened. When they lost the cow, they had to find another way to survive. Therefore, they began to cultivate the fields. This gave them food, but also surpluses to sell at the market. So they had bought not one, but three other cows, plus chickens, rabbits and ducks. Since then, prosperity had arrived.

The young monk then understood that breaking the small ties that give us security can be the first step in freeing ourselves from a prison that prevents us from growing. What can you conclude from this? Only one thing: the universe is yours. Go get him.

THANK YOU

From the bottom of my heart I want to thank you for buying my book.

You could have chosen from many other books, but you decided to take a chance and choose mine.

So thank you again for buying this book and for reading it lovingly to the end. I put a lot of love into each of its leaves.

Before you go, I wanted to ask you a small favor.

Could you consider posting a review on the platform? Publishing a review is the best and easiest way to support the work of independent authors like me, who seek to capture our knowledge in these sheets and make life a little easier for our readers.

Your comments will help me continue to grow as a freelance writer and I will also be able to know the type of books that will help you get the results you want. It would mean a lot to me to hear from you.

>> Leave a review on Amazon.com

ABOUT HE AUTHOR

Ollie Snider is a writer with a passion for personal growth and the development of the mind. His career as a writer focuses on self-help books and his main objective is to help people achieve their full potential through knowledge. It seeks to contribute a grain of sand to the vast sea of human knowledge.

In addition to being a full-time writer, Ollie is a proud father of a family who thanks his loved ones every day for the unconditional love they give him. His dedication to his family and his passion for writing have led him to inspire thousands of people worldwide.

Made in the USA
Las Vegas, NV
17 September 2023

77702257R00069